THE HIGH ALTITUDE VIEW

How to Gain Perspective to Grow Your Practice

Steven Plewes, ChFC, CPC, ELI-MP

All rights reserved. This book or parts thereof may not be reproduced in any form, stored in any retrieval system, or transmitted in any form by any means—electronic, mechanical, photocopy, recording, or otherwise—without prior written permission of the publisher, except as provided by United States of America copyright law. For permission requests, write to the publisher, at "Attention: Permissions Coordinator," at the address below.
Coachplewes@gmail.com

Although the author and publisher have made every effort to ensure that the information in this book was correct at press time, the author and publisher do not assume and hereby disclaim any liability to any party for any loss, damage, or disruption caused by errors or omissions, whether such errors or omissions result from negligence, accident, or any other cause.

Visit the author's website at www.steveplewes.com.

Cover design, interior formatting and graphics by Studio92, LLC.
www.studio92.us

Copyright © 2019 by Steven Plewes
HCC Publishing
ISBN: 9781094963891

Dedication

This book is dedicated to those who know deep down inside that they have more to learn, more to do, and more to give, and who desperately want to reach their full potential for what it can mean for themselves, others they care about, and those they love.

Praise for *The High Altitude View*

"The key to success in business is to make sure you are successful in LIFE as a whole. Steve Plewes has mastered both and is now sharing his hard-earned wisdom with you. His creativity is unmatched in the financial services profession, and now he channels that through his coaching of financial professionals. I've known Steve for more than 30 years and he has been a friend, a fellow volunteer in MDRT, and more importantly, a mentor for me. Now that he has chosen to become a full-time coach, he is coaching and mentoring both of my sons. If you don't like the book, he will refund your money 10 times over so go ahead and buy 100…you can't lose."

Brian D. Heckert, CLU, ChFC
CEO and Founder FSM Wealth
2016 Million Dollar Round Table President
Nashville, IL

"During my 30 years in business I've read a lot of books. With the odd exception, I've found very few that had the sort of impact that could take me from 'here' to 'there.'

What makes Steve Plewes' books relevant, insightful, and results-focused is his practical experience, personal successes, and his wonderful communication style. It is, in my opinion, a 'must-read' for anyone really serious about success."

Sandro Forte
Million Dollar Round Table Member and 21-year Top of the Table Member Speaker, Author, Podcaster
London, England

"This is a must read, learn, ask, and act book that will deeply affect your life and those you choose to serve. Steve's words of wisdom come from the inside where the reality of humanity exists – one's soul. Steve authentically shares his journey of self-acceptance that has led to his personal and professional success. You will be inspired to ask questions and learn more of yourself and your clients. And by doing so, whether in defeat or victory, you will experience the richness of life that is truly life with *The High Altitude View*!"

John F. Nichols MSM, CLU
Partner, Insurance Wholesale Solutions
2013-14 National Association of Insurance and Financial Advisors, President
Million Dollar Round Table and Top of the Table Member
Chicago, IL

"Some people succeed in our business, some people write books on how to succeed in our business. Just occasionally someone who has really succeeded writes a really good book telling the rest of the world 'how.' Such a person is Steve Plewes and such a book is *The High Altitude View*. Read it, put what it says into practice; it will give anyone who does the path to follow to achieve real success."

Tony Gordon
2001 Million Dollar Round Table President
Bristol, England

"Alexander Graham Bell once said, 'When one door closes, another opens; but we often look so long and so regretfully upon the closed door that we do not see the one which has opened for us.' In this book, Steve Plewes shares his insights, gained through many years on the front lines in the financial advisory world, as well as in his coaching career. Let Steve help you close doors that have limited your potential, and open new doors to a different and exciting way to look at yourself, your career, your client interactions, and the value you bring to your relationships.

"I've been very fortunate to have a front-row seat with Steve along his journey. Steve has been a mentor, business associate, and most importantly, a great friend for many years. His unique ability is that of a great communicator. First communicating with his clients to build a successful financial services practice and now Steve has upped his game by helping others refine their vision and purpose, and then clarifying their value. Now the time has come for you to up your game as well. Sit back and enjoy. It's going to change the way you think!"

Edward C. Skelly, CLU, ChFC, RICP, RFC
President & Founder
Sterling Financial Partners
Million Dollar Round Table and Top of the Table Member
Sterling, VA

"What got you to where you are today won't get you to where you want to go tomorrow. Complacency and doing things the way you have always done them in the past will no longer serve you well moving into the future. Today's fast-paced environment calls for trusted advisors to think and act differently. Steve's book, *The High Altitude View*, illustrates how embracing a new mindset can change your world, and that of your clients. This book is a must read in order for you to reach a higher level of happiness and success."

Jennifer Borislow, CLU
President, Borislow Insurance
2012 Million Dollar Round Table President
Methuen, MA

"A definition of success that meant the most to me during my career is, 'Success in life is the ratio of what you are to what you might have been.' For you mathematicians in the reading audience, Steve has illustrated in this book what he has learned during his nearly 40-year career as a financial advisor, that the ratio of 'What he is, divided by what he was capable of' approached 1/1.

"So read, take to heart, and apply his recommendations and you, too, will become the business success of which YOU are capable."

James E. Rogers, CLU, CFP
James E. Rogers, Ltd.
2008 Million Dollar Round Table President
Vancouver, Canada

"In a financial world that has become increasingly digitized, where an advisor's 'value proposition' is nakedly questioned, Steve's thoughts, expressed in a straightforward, forceful, but humble way refresh the necessary 'humanity' of the advisor/client relationship and remind us of the simple things we can do to find our way."

Brian H. Ashe, CLU
Brian Ashe & Associates
2000 Million Dollar Round Table President
2012 John Newton Russell Award Recipient
Chicago, IL

"There are many books on mindset out there that are filled with platitudes and fluff. With *The High Altitude View*, Steve has written a blueprint that takes his reader through an awakening experience step-by-step. After reading it, I was ready to not just compete but to dominate. The way he breaks down the inner energy blocks was a game-changer for me moving forward. Confidence is an internal knowing that we can manifest whatever we truly put our minds to. It would be disrespectful to your future self if you didn't read this transformational book from start to finish."

Bruce Lund, PhD
Founder & Director
90-Day Sales Manager™
Denver, CO

"Many books are written by producers or motivational speakers who never became great advisors. Over a 40-year career, Steve Plewes became a great advisor. Steve is one of those gifted producers who are both equally creative and practical. He has written an easy to read book about how to achieve the most difficult goal for any great advisor: to only work from the High Altitude View. Whether we are at the beginning or in the twilight of our careers, we should never stop learning. Steve's simple, transferable ideas can help you grow towards attaining real success in our great profession. But you must possess the WANT TO: because nothing happens unless you want it to happen. Every producer should read this book!"

Julian H. Good, Jr. CLU, ChFC, AEP
Good Financial Group, LLC
2011 Million Dollar Round Table President
New Orleans, LA

"Steve's book, *The High Altitude View*, is right on point. If you want to get to the next level of success and professionalism, follow the guidelines he has detailed and explained in his book. Steve shares his personal story as a leader in the financial services industry and utilizes his perspective as a coach to help you become a leader and reach your full potential in the financial services industry as well."

Marvin H. Feldman, CLU, ChFC, RFC
Feldman Financial Group
2002 Million Dollar Round Table President
2011 John Newton Russell Award Recipient
Palm Harbor, FL

"The power and importance of our mindset, belief systems, and habits either empower our success or limit our full potential. Steve's insights, revealed in this book, are unique due to his personal experience, successes, and history of studying how our beliefs hold us back or set us free. You should pay attention to his book, *The High Altitude View*, because you will be learning from someone who has DONE IT. Simply put, it is tried and true wisdom."

Mark Schoenbeck, CFP®
Executive Vice President, National Sales
Kestra Financial
Austin, TX

"Having known Steve Plewes for a number of years, I am delighted he finally decided to share his experience and insights with all of us by writing this book. Whether we are at a challenging point in our careers or simply enjoy learning from others, Steve's book has a lot to offer us. Only someone like Steve, who has worked through so many situations covered in this book, can truly pass on the wisdom to help others to grow."

Caroline Banks FPFS
Caroline Banks & Associates Ltd.
2015 Million Dollar Round Table President
London, England

"I have known Steve Plewes for many years, not just as a successful Top of the Table advisor, but also as a mentor and a great leader. His book, *The High Altitude View*, will help not only newer agents and advisors, but also anyone who wants to achieve a higher level of success. In his book he shows you, through his personal experiences, how a shift in your mindset and a change of perspective can improve your sales performance as well as increase your happiness in life."

我認識 Steve Plewes 多年，他是一位成功的財務策劃顧問，也是一位導師和偉大的領導者。Steve 的新書《The High Altitude View》不僅可以幫助新一代的代理和顧問，也可以幫助各位擴闊視野，獲得更高的成就。這本書能夠啟發你如何通過個人經歷打開思維的視野，提高績效及增加生活上的幸福感。

我认识 Steve Plewes 多年，他是一位成功的财务策划顾问，也是一位导师和伟大的领导者。Steve 的新书《The High Altitude View》不仅可以帮助新一代的代理和顾问，也可以帮助各位扩阔视野，获得更高的成就。这本书能够启发你如何通过个人经历打开思维的视野，提高绩效及增加生活上的幸福感。

Pecky Wong So Ping
Million Dollar Round Table and Top of the Table Member
Hong Kong

"Steve Plewes has been a leader in the financial services industry for nearly 40 years. He is now sharing his knowledge and experience to save you many years of 'on the job training.' If you read this book and APPLY it to your life, there is no doubt in my mind that you will excel in this business. Steve will literally FAST TRACK you to the top!"

Tom Hegna, CLU, ChFC, CASL, LACP
Best Selling Author, International Speaker
Fountain Hills, AZ

"Steve's book, The High Altitude View, contains the exact knowledge and tools that advisors and firms need in order to take their practices and firms to the next level. Thank you, Steve, for providing this road map to the thousands of financial advisors who can practically implement these tools and strategies. Our firm has benefited from Steve's coaching and now, thanks to this book, we have additional training and expertise to complement that coaching."

Albert P Herzog III, MBA, ChFC, CFP®
Founder & Director
Executive Wealth Management
Brighton, MI

The High Altitude View

How to Gain Perspective to Grow Your Practice

Foreword xv

Introduction xx

Chapter 1—Success and What it Really Means 1

Chapter 2—Inner Obstacles to Success 11

Chapter 3—Seven Levels of Attitudinal Perspective 27

Chapter 4—Six Mindsets of Success 39

Chapter 5—Shifting Your Mindset to The High Altitude View 55

Chapter 6—Managing Your Mindset 69

Chapter 7—Goal Setting and Other Tools 83

Chapter 8—With Change Comes Challenges 95

Chapter 9—Your New Mindset and Leadership 109

Chapter 10—You've Earned the Right to Have High Altitude
    Conversations 125

Acknowledgements 143

About the Author 147

Foreword

This book is about change—change of the heart and change of the mind.

William Faulkner wrote the phrase, "Be better than yourself," and I hope that you're ready to be just that. It is an honor to welcome you aboard. You're in for the journey of a lifetime; however, the person reading this Foreword may not think or act like the person finishing the last chapter. This book will help you grow and go up to the next level—if you ardently desire to get there.

Steve Plewes is a great salesperson who became a great advisor who became a great coach. You are going to be learning from one of the best. I know this because we have cheered each other on at the high end of the financial services profession for more than 25 years.

I liked Steve the moment I met him; he wears well, has an easy sensibility, and has a great sense of humor.

Do you know the difference between cuddling and holding someone down so that they can't get away? Good! You have social intelligence. The more you have, the easier it is to grow.

Meeting and advising people at the high end is a combination of social intelligence and percentages.

This book, if taken to heart, will help you get out of your own way. A lot of self-help books tend to make simple things complicated and almost mysterious. But the purpose of this fine book is the opposite of that. Steve has written an owner's manual for the financial advisor who wants to make a quantum leap.

Great advisors are made, not born. Advising at the high end is a learned behavior. The move from poor advisor to good adviser is difficult; there are too many moving parts that do not always line up.

With the right thinking and a little tweaking, however, the good advisor can become a great advisor. That is why you are holding this book, and I encourage you to daydream about what you will feel like when great things start happening in your life in general and your career in particular. This is not part of a "to do" list, it is part of a "to be" list.

Daydream hard while you enjoy this book, and stop taking yourself so seriously. The path you are on is not a prison sentence; it is a life blessed with a brand new attitude helping people who not only want to know you better, they want to work with you on a much more meaningful level.

One of the reasons the card game Bridge still fascinates people is that, in order to be relatively good at it, you must be willing to be totally flummoxed by it while you are learning to play. The same is true in advising others at the high end.

If you already happen to be successful in meeting and advising great clients, congratulations! Kindly remember, no one is so successful that he or she doesn't need to be inspired. If you are feeling tired, exasperated, and down to your last ounce of human juice, this book will help you get back on track. If you are too experienced to be a beginner—and perhaps too good to be temporarily unsuccessful—this book will help you pull yourself back up to your full height. What Steve has written will inspire you, not motivate you—it will *inspire* you. Motivation lasts about two minutes; inspiration can last a lifetime.

My wife thinks I'm nosey. At least that is what she keeps writing in her diary. What would your best clients write in their diary about you? About your attitude? What would the person in the next office say about your skill set? How would they describe you? How would you like to be married to you?

The late classy movie star Cary Grant once said, "A thousand details add up to one impression." What impression of yourself do you hold right now?

A leader is someone people follow, even when they don't have to. Leaders lift others up. A leader looks for growth the same way a person looks for a piece of lost jewelry. On occasion, you have witnessed people lead from in front. Now it's your turn.

Great advisors are highly disciplined. They are willing to do something today in the hope they may get results a year or more from now. I am emphasizing the word "may" because prospecting for great people to advise requires a lot of faith. Let your wife or husband know what you are reading and talk about it. Write your own unvarnished observations and upbeat hopes in the margins of this book.

Remember, this is your manual for change; the person finishing this book will be different from the person starting it. This won't be your old self; it will be something quite a bit better.

Andrew Jackson was quoted as saying, "One person with courage is a majority." You can be that person, a committee of one, with the help of many when you are challenged.

Get ready; it's coming. If you are giving advice at the high end you will be challenged by prospects, clients, other advisors, and people to whom you report and people who report to you. Buckle up; this can be tough—wear a helmet. Steve will help you remember to take the long view and that the journey –on some days—is meant to be challenging. It is also joyful.

You will grow. The sun will rise tomorrow. Things will look better in the morning.

A person's faith will grow in direct proportion to the size of a problem or opportunity. Optimism is an intellectual choice. Anything else is mental illness (take this from Doctor Brennan). Most successful people are optimistic by nature. Not everybody, mind you—just the happy ones.

Jack Canfield and Mark Victor Hansen, the wonderful authors of the series of *Chicken Soup for the Soul* books, tell the story of people running into the office of W. Clement Stone yelling, "Mr. Stone, we have a problem!" Stone, a serial optimist, would always reply, "No, we have an opportunity. Now, tell me about our opportunity."

You will be given an opportunity to grow every time you pick up this book.

Winston Churchill knew what he was talking about when he said, "Success is moving from failure to failure without the loss of enthusiasm." No truer words were ever spoken.

People who do well in this life occupy a different space than most. Leaders don't want—or expect—an easy hand dealt to them; they prefer a lousy hand played well. Not everyone understands this kind of thinking; you will after you've finished this book.

Adversity in small doses builds character if an advisor takes the road less traveled. Happiness is a choice, not the result of how life treats us.

To live this way, a person needs wisdom. In order to have wisdom, however, a person will usually need humility. What does humility look like? Find a person who is thankful. This can be called rational optimism or emotional bravery; it is only this deeply held belief that gives a person the genuine feeling of positive intent.

Positive intent is the emotional capital to build a big life.

Advising others at the high end was never meant to humiliate great advisors—just identify them.

People believe in optimists, even when they might not believe in themselves. A woman who believes in her husband makes him believe in himself. A man who believes in his wife makes her believe in herself. A client who believes in his or her advisor makes the advisor believe in himself or herself. An advisor who believes in his or her client makes the client believe in himself or herself.

Before I leave you and all the new discoveries you will make, you might be wondering, "Will I owe anything to anyone?"

Actually, two things.

First, it is your assignment to help at least one other person grow the way you will.

Second, if you like this book, please buy one for a friend.

If you don't like it, nobody ever got hurt keeping their opinion to themselves.

Be well the road.

D. Scott Brennan
2016 John Newton Russell Memorial Award Winner
Million Dollar Round Table Past-President
South Bend, Indiana

Introduction

"Son, no matter how successful you become, never forget that you were born in the shallow end of the gene pool!"

That was always our family joke. As if anyone from our family had ever become successful, or at least successful by any notion of what we thought of as success: fame, financial independence, true wealth. Oh sure, there was the one uncle who had married into money, or at least into the hope of a large inheritance. But otherwise, no one in our family, going back generations, had really done anything very noteworthy other than work hard, make ends meet, and keep things going. And there is certainly nothing wrong with that.

The one thing that stands out in my family, though, is that almost every one of my relatives was either in business for themselves or in sales. So it's not that surprising that I ended up going into sales and owning my own business. Inheriting the family's entrepreneurial DNA was a true gift to me, but I also inherited generations of limiting beliefs that came along with that entrepreneurism. And I believe that one of my greatest accomplishments was learning to overcome those limiting beliefs and break through the barriers to success that had eluded my family for generations.

I'm not saying that people in my family weren't happy or that anyone was destitute. Success can be measured in many ways. And if I think about it, growing up in a modest home surrounded by a community of people with varying levels of work ethic was probably a very healthy thing for me. Importantly, it showed me many examples of the cause and effect of effort versus reward.

I share this information with you at the outset of this book because I want to make a point I don't want you to miss. Most people I have encountered in life have had a similar experience as mine but have chosen different ways to cope with and learn from their life experiences. Some simply followed the same path as their family before them. Others chose to break out of the legacy of those limiting beliefs and strive to do something significant with their lives. Some soared. Some crashed and burned. The key lies in how a person chooses to see and overcome their challenges. And please know, we all have challenges.

In writing this book, my hope is that you will benefit from, be motivated by, and maybe even be inspired by the stories, ideas, and concepts that lie within these pages. Over the past 40 plus years of my life, I have struggled, failed, failed, and struggled again. I have been incredibly lucky and, at times, almost unbelievably unlucky. I have been blessed to have so many mentors and great influences in my life who have shown me the example of how to do things the right way. And I also had a few people who have shown me what the wrong way looked like. And almost always, my most significant hurdle was my own limiting beliefs, assumptions, interpretations, and toxic self-talk. It wasn't until I actually gave myself permission to succeed that success finally showed up.

I hope that, by my sharing the beliefs that I have developed, the mistakes that I have made, and the lessons that I've learned—sometimes the hard way—you will be able to accelerate your own success, whatever that looks like for you. Because what has developed out of my life experience is that my true passion has become helping other people move forward in life.

This book represents the fundamental and foundational beliefs of all my business and coaching experiences. The stories, techniques, and concepts that I will share come from my own personal experiences as I moved from average to exceptional, from mediocre producer to the Top of the Table. The ideas and concepts presented here will help anyone in the financial services business who is trying to break out of his or her comfort zone to achieve the success and happiness that he or she truly wants out of life.

Maybe the most important lesson I have learned in my life is also one of the last important lessons I have learned. If I had it to do all over again, I would have spent way more time figuring out and owning *who I am*. Who am I and what are my values? What are my boundaries? What will I tolerate, and what are my metrics for assessing success? It's ironic really. After I figured out the answers to these questions, my life purpose really started to come into focus and success came quickly.

In the late 1990s, I was involved in a coaching program for entrepreneurs. One of the exercises that we conducted early in the process was sending a letter to my top clients to ask for their input regarding a very important element of our relationship. I felt a bit uncomfortable doing this for several reasons, not the least of which was I wasn't sure I wanted to hear their answers! Prior to this project, I used to come into a meeting with a prospect or client with reams of paper containing so many third-party references about what I was proposing or presenting to them that they would just know I was knowledgeable about the subject. At least that was my reasoning. But this material was just a cloak to hide behind, because my self-confidence was so low that I needed something to ward off the questions that I was afraid they would ask and that I assumed I wouldn't be able to answer.

When I sent the letter to my top clients, I let them know that I was conducting a project for the coaching program in which I was participating, and that I had one single question to ask them: "What is the one unique ability that you feel that I bring to our relationship?"

That's a simple question, really. The answer I received from the 95% of clients who responded was some variation of the following:

- "We knew the minute that we met you that we could trust you."

- "I knew within the first two minutes of talking with you that you were someone I could trust."

- "I just knew in my heart that you were a person who would look out for me and put my interest first."

Wow! I was blown away to say the least. What people told me was that without my even trying, without a ream of paper containing third-party material, without any prompting, that they saw me and pretty much instantly trusted me! Can you imagine what that did to my self-confidence? It literally changed my life! But most importantly, it also changed how I viewed myself. And it set into motion a series of changes as to how I approached people in all walks of life and how I began to conduct my business going forward. It changed my perception of my self.

Perception is such a powerful concept. How we see our selves, how we see the world, how we interpret situations, and the assumptions we make all come from how we perceive that which we see. In fact, it isn't overstating it to say that how you see anything is how you see everything.

Okay, so what does all this have to do with success in the financial services business, you ask. Well, in my experience, this business comes down to relationships with and among people—people we work with and work for. Our business is filled with prospects who offer sales resistance, clients who hold expectations, compliance departments and underwriters and their demands. And of course there are the vendors, whose support we sometimes rely upon, and our company managers and office associates. The list goes on and on, and I haven't even mentioned family and friends.

We clearly must understand all those people to relate well to them, but most of all, we need a good, clear, honest understanding of our selves, because it all starts there.

How we define who we are, what we want, and why we want it are fundamental to achieving success. But for each and every one of us, there are obstacles and hurdles and roadblocks along the road to that success. Understanding your outer and inner blocks, your perceptions, and your limiting beliefs will be instrumental in achieving what you want. Becoming more self-aware and becoming a stronger self-manager will help you build your investment philosophy and your belief systems around the products you sell—investments or insurance.

Self-awareness will be key to developing your value proposition, which is perhaps the most import element of a successful financial services career. Knowing your true value and being confident in that value—and being able to communicate it artfully to your clients and prospects—will elevate you above the impending sameness that is settling into this profession. Being able to skillfully manage the sales process and learning to elevate the conversation to the highest altitude view of things will separate you from the average advisor who reacts to questions and objections around price, product, and performance.

The high-altitude advisor approaches and advises people with a wisdom based mentality and helps the prospect and client discover his or her *why*. And as an advisor, when you help people discover *their* why, you will then discover *your* why.

There are so many subtleties that contribute to success in the sales and advisory world. Soft skills are often overlooked in favor of strong closing techniques. At times we say things without even listening to what we say, and we listen too little. Understanding the power of the words we use and when to use them can be transformative. Breaking away from conventional thinking and taking a 360 degree walk around challenges with your clients can help your clients begin to see you as a creative problem-solver.

In this book, I will share with you how I communicate challenging subjects with clients and the deliberate and powerful word choices I make. I will reveal the mindsets that I have adopted that have transformed my small practice into a multimillion-dollar advisory firm. And in this book, I will teach you how to overcome your limiting beliefs, change your perceptions, and manage your self-talk so that you can become very clear about who you are, what you have to offer your clients and prospects, and what your personal definition of success looks like for you. Mostly, I will share with you the most important lessons, tools, and techniques that have helped me to get out of my own way, to break out of my comfort zone, to learn how to fail, and to become more comfortable with releasing control to become an influencer to the people who have trusted me along this journey.

I wish that I had read a book like this 25 years ago, and I am both deeply grateful and happy that you are reading it today!

Steven Plewes, ChFC, CPC, ELI-MP

CHAPTER 1

Success and What it Really Means

"Define success on your own terms, achieve it by your own rules, and build a life you're proud to live."

– Anne Sweeney

What Does Success Look Like to You?

One of my least favorite words in the English language is "should." When I hear this word I instantly feel boxed in. Maybe it's just me, or the way that I'm "wired," but when I hear the word I actually have a physical reaction to it. To me, the word "should" represents someone else's idea of what is supposed to be or what is supposed to happen. It feels so judgmental to me, and if there is one thing that really stops me cold, it's when I am feeling judged.

"You know, you should go into the office every day."

"If you want to make more money, you should make more calls."

"If a client wants to see you after hours, you really should accommodate them."

The list of examples goes on . . .

When I hear someone say something like, "You should" or "You need to," it feels to me like if I don't do it his or her way, then my way is wrong. Now maybe I am interpreting this the wrong way, but I'm just sharing how it makes me feel. And it's not like my way is always the best way, but it is my way.

When it comes to defining success, how often have we bought into other people's ideas of what that is or what that might look like? Likely, we've done that quite often, because for many people, we just haven't taken the time to really consider what success means to us. And often the definitions that are out there sound pretty good, after all—big car, big house, lots of money, good health, fame, *things* of various kinds! But those things may not be what are really important to you and may or may not motivate you at your core. And likely, if they are not really important to you, you will give up eventually, because accomplishing goals not tied to your core values will leave you empty and unhappy. Take it from me. Been there, done that!

It's very important that you take the time to discover and define what success is to you, because this definition is what you will use to measure and assess your progress. Your definition of success ideally will be tied to your core values. By core values, I am talking about those values that are fundamental to you as a person, the values and beliefs that are at your "core." After all, these values are where you most naturally will focus your efforts, good or bad. In other words, if having lots of money is important to you, then you will make decisions that point you toward that value. If having more work-life balance in your life is an important value, then you will make decisions that drive you toward that value. That's why it's so important that you take stock of what values are truly important to you, so that you can focus your time, energy, and resources toward goals built around those values.

What is success then? What is it for you? If someone were to ask you to define success, what would you say? I know what success is for me. And after I took the time to really consider what was truly important to me and defined my most important values, my personal life and my work life got a whole lot less complicated. Because after I defined what I really wanted, what was truly important to me according to my values, it also became quite clear what wasn't important, and I was able to stop wasting time on those things that didn't keep me on track to where I wanted to go.

I'll share a story with you. In 1997, I began participating in The Strategic Coach™ program. This is a coaching program for entrepreneurs, in which I stayed for five years. One of the first things we did was take time to set our life goals. I set five large life goals. And I tell you this story for a couple of reasons. First, I hope I will spark some ideas for you and motivate you to set some life goals that you can begin to work toward. And second, I will show what large goals can look like.

I set five life goals. You may set more or less, but five seems like a good number to me.

The number one goal I set was to stay married to my wife for the rest of my life. Now, I'm not going to say this was the easiest goal I ever set. And it probably wasn't that easy for her either, but we've been married 40 years as of September, 2018. My uncle (the one that married into money) was fond of saying, "Just remember that the first 50 years of marriage are the hardest," so I feel like we're making progress.

But seriously, we have a wonderful marriage and we have three beautiful children and four amazing grandchildren. So while we've had a lot of fun, we also have experienced the usual challenges life throws at you—joys and tragedies, failures and successes. I am so fortunate to have married my best friend and someone who I enjoy spending lots of time with and who shares the same core values as me. And that may be the key to a successful marriage or any successful relationship for that matter.

The second goal I set was that I wanted to remain physically fit into my old age. And the jury's still out on that, but I'm hanging in there so far. It's a priority for me to remain physically fit. I think it's important because I've seen people when they get in their 60s; it's kind of an inflection point where one decides whether they want to be fit or whether they want to be unfit and unhealthy. Staying healthy is important simply because you can live longer. And if you have clear reasons to live and if you have some big goals, then why not just keep going if you can? I just want you to get a glimpse of this mindset, the mindset that says, "Hey, we set some big goals and we have good reasons to get up every day. And if we can remove the obstacles in our way then we can go after pretty much anything we want."

And why wouldn't we? Why don't we?

The third goal I set was that I wanted to educate our kids all the way through college, because not everybody in our family got to go to college. So that was very important to me. I wanted all three of our kids to go through at least undergrad, which they all did.

The fourth goal was that I wanted to be financially independent by the time I was 58 years old. And I got pretty close to achieving that goal on time; it actually was two years later, when I was 60.

The fifth goal was that I wanted to have a second career, after my career in financial services, based on skills that I acquired in my first career. Honestly, I wasn't sure exactly what that was going to be at the time I set the goal. I love photography. I love music. But I love people more than anything. And I am passionate about helping people move forward in life, which was the key element of my financial practice and the relationships that I built there. Coaching, writing, and public speaking eventually found me, and it suits me well and I enjoy it, because it's a great way to continue to help people move forward in life.

Who Are You?

I really want you to focus on your personal definition of success. I want you to think about what it is that would make you feel successful, not what others say it "should" be.

To be able to define this properly, though, you first have to ask yourself, "Who am I really?"

And who you really are has to do with your values. We tend to think of ourselves in terms of, and even *as*, our role. We tend to think of ourselves as financial advisors or as a father or as a mother. Whatever we are, we tend to think of ourselves in terms of our role, but I encourage you to think in terms of *your values* instead. In a sense, you *are* your values. Your values have a lot to do with how you see the world and where you focus your energy. This is important because when you get to a place where you can just show up and your values are aligned—and that's who you are—it makes many of your life decisions very, very easy. When you know exactly who you are, what you will do and won't do, what you accept and what you don't accept, and what your boundaries are, you can be very focused. And when you are focused, many of those obstacles that tend to get in the way of your success and happiness no longer will stop you.

So, who are you?

Think values. Are you creative? Are you a caring person? Are you ambitious? Think about what is important to you in terms of value definitions, your values. If somebody were to describe you, what would they say? For me, I'm a creative person. I have a sense of humor. I'm caring. I'm a very intuitive person. I feel things. I feel my way through life, so I have to work with that, because some people are just pure thinkers, and they're more analytical and logical.

The more you know about who you are and what you bring to the table, the more authentic you can become, and the more you can show up in front of your clients and in your communities and with your families as authentic to who you really are. When you can do that, you're on track to really having happiness and achieving success.

What Do You Want?

After you know who you are, you then have to think deeply about what it is that you really want. What you want is your values-based goal. After all, all I'm really talking about here is honestly answering the questions of who are you, what do you want, and why do you want it. So, what do you want? What are your goals based on your values?

I wrote earlier about my five big goals, which are the things that I wanted. I call these high-altitude goals. When defining your own goals, feel free to make them more short-term goals, if that's what makes sense for you. If you're striving to qualify for the Million Dollar Round Table (MDRT) for the first time, fine. Or maybe you want to reach the Top of the Table. Whatever your goal might be, just define what it is that you want.

Right now, write down a couple things that would be important to you, in your life, in the short-term, mid-term, or long-term.

Why Do You Want It?

After you are clear about who you are and what you want, then it's crucial to define why you want what you want. It's very important that we know why we want something. Your why is your values-based purpose. Is it for the money? Is it for the financial security? Is it for the ego? Is it for the status? Is it for the sense of accomplishment? Is it to please someone else? What is your why?

In Simon Sinek's transformational book *Start with Why*, he argues that knowing your why is not about inventing something, but rather it is a process of discovery. It makes sense when you think about it. How many times have you been caught up in activities, projects, and even some relationships, and when things aren't going well you catch yourself asking, "Why am I even doing this?"

In the world of a financial advisor, it's probably easy to think of ten things with which you are currently involved that do not align with your values-based purpose – or in other words, your why. That's why Sinek says it's a process of discovery. Stop and think about what's important about the activities, projects, and relationships in your life that are not currently aligned with your purpose according to your core values. That would be a great place to start to understand what you really stand for.

When you understand who you are and what you're all about, you will become very comfortable in your own skin. And when comfortable, you can show up in any situation and say, "This is who I am. This is what I want to do. And this is why I want to do it."

Everything becomes clear and well-defined. When you know who you are, that knowledge becomes your foundation for everything. And when you know what you want, that desire becomes your mission. The *why* becomes your fuel, the source of your passion. That's where the passion comes from. This understanding makes life much simpler, because if you know exactly what you want and you know why you want it, then you can build all your systems around that. All your decisions come back to that, and anything that tries to get into your thinking that is contrary becomes just a distraction.

It's a distraction because it doesn't measure up with who you are—the boundaries that you set for yourself, the values that you put in place, the characteristics that you recognize about yourself—and it doesn't match up with your why. Removing the distractions, or non-value aligned activities, makes life easier, especially during those times when you're so busy and your resources are just tapped out.

I hear people say all the time, "We're just so busy." But why are they so busy? Perhaps it's because they're holding on to things they shouldn't. Or maybe they're avoiding some things. Maybe they're trying to validate themselves in different ways. Maybe they are clutching tightly to control.

But after you become crystal clear about who you are, what you want, and why you want it, you then will have the foundation to truly focus, let go of certain things, start moving toward the goals that are aligned with your core values, and really grow.

Your *who* is your foundation. It's based on your core values. That's the starting point. Who you are is defined by what struggles you are willing to endure, what difficulties you are willing to tolerate, and what boundaries you are willing to set.

Your *what* is your mandate. It's your mission. What you want will be defined not only by your desires, but by what pain you are willing to suffer and what is most important to you according to your values.

And your *why* is where the passion comes from. It's the fuel that helps you accomplish your goals.

All actions taken will be driven by what you naturally feel is most important to you and what you will be willing to fight for at all costs.

The passion that comes from that fight is going to propel you through your inner blocks. It's going to remove those barriers for you on your way to achieving *your* next level of success—the next level of success according to *your* definition.

Before Moving On, Ask Yourself...

1. What does success look like for you?

___

2. What are the core values by which you will measure your success?

___

3. What is your sense of God's unique purpose for your life?

___

CHAPTER 2

Inner Obstacles to Success

"Energy and persistence conquer all things."
– Benjamin Franklin

What's Stopping You?

I've already talked about some of the challenges keeping you from the success you want, but now I'm going to get into some real internal obstacles. Even after you are clear about who you are, what you want, and why you want it, you still have three significant obstacles that you can run up against.

First is your perception of your self—how you view yourself and how you think.

Second is how you view the world around you. Your perceptions of the world and how you react to situations in life, especially when you are under stress, can create chaos and distract you from your mission.

This second issue is a big one. How you react under stress and how you show up throughout the day affects your energy levels and has a huge impact on your productivity. What's this about energy? Well, most people intuitively know what energy is. You know when a high-energy or positive-energy person comes into a room and they kind of just light up the room. And on the flip side, don't you know that person who comes in the room and just sucks the energy right out of everyone? That's the low-energy, or worse, negative-energy person.

So you likely already know something about energy and how it can affect you. You know good energy and you know bad energy. And you know the effect each can have on people in terms of attraction or rejection.

The third potential obstacle depends on your ability to manage your mindset. Are you willing to let go of some of the thoughts that you just always believed were true? This is an important question to answer, because the thinking that got you where you are may not be the thinking you need to get you to where you're going. You likely got where you are because you're locked into some particular thinking, which is both good and bad. I am referring mostly to things that you have learned. But you can learn new things, and you can adopt new habits and practices. *Warning: It is not always easy to let go of old habits or old thinking.*

Energy Blocks*

So how do you see yourself and how do you think? Well, there are two primary things that we're going to talk about in this area. The first is called energy blocks. Energy blocks sap your energy. They keep you away from opportunity. Let's dig in, and I think you'll see what I mean.

The GAILs

Let's start with the set of four energy blocks we most commonly deal with in coaching. They are called the GAILs.* The first GAIL is your Gremlin. The Gremlin is just a cute little word used to get you to think about that inner critic that all people have—that toxic self-talk that we all hear. That critic says things like this:

- "You're not good enough."

- "You're not lovable."

- "You're not ready."

- "You don't have enough education."

- "You don't deserve success."

The Gremlin usually comes out whenever you have an opportunity and you're really excited about doing something. It also comes out when you're breaking out of your comfort zone. And it pops up when you start to get into that growth mindset. In these situations and myriad others like them, all of a sudden, there it is. The Gremlin shows up saying, "No, you're not doing that. You're not going to make that sale. You're not going to get that opportunity because you're not good enough. Whoever told you that you could do that?"

This is your inner self-talk. All people naturally have this. What you have to do is just recognize that when you start to have these thoughts, you recognize them for what they are—just thoughts. They are not real. They are not true. You have to move past your natural reaction by saying, "I hear you talking to me, Gremlin, but I'm not going to pay attention. I'm not going to buy into what you're trying to tell me. I'm going to move past that."

The fact that your Gremlin may pop up in your head at a time when you are trying to do something significant or move out of your comfort zone is absolute confirmation that what you're trying to do is *what you are supposed to be doing.* It seems ironic, but if you're getting negative messages in your self-talk that tell you that you shouldn't be doing something, that's 100% confirmation that you *should* be doing it, and that it's going to stretch you and grow you.

So what is your inner critic saying to you? What do you hear? Take note of your inner self-talk and work on your responses.

The "A" in GAILS stands for Assumptions. When something has happened in the past and therefore you believe that it'll happen again in the future, that's the kind of assumption I am talking about here.

How many times has this come up for you? You've tried something, and it failed, and then the opportunity to try it again comes up, and you say to yourself, "Hmmm . . . I did that already. I tried that. I know that's not going to work, so I'm just not going to even try it again."

Frankly, I consider that a small-scale failure. This is just a mindset where you're telling yourself, "Hey, I already tried that. It doesn't work, so what's the point?"

And what you've done when you lock yourself down like that is you've created a barrier for yourself, keeping yourself from moving forward in that particular incident, and not getting what you really want. Even if your goal is a small one, assumptions can have a large negative impact.

Consider the example of one of my coaching clients, who was just desperate to get out of the office. He knew instinctively that he needed to be out and in front of people more. By the way, he's very successful by anybody's standard. He is a Top of the Table producer. But he was very frustrated because he wanted to stop being in the office so much.

Even though he wanted to stay out of the office, he felt compelled to go in every day. If he didn't go in, he felt guilty. So somehow, he's taught himself that's what work is. (Note the limiting belief!). Somebody told him somewhere along the line that if he's not in the office, he's not actually working. And the worst part of it was that when I really challenged him, I found out that what he was really worried about was what his employees were going to say about him if he didn't come in.

He had made lots of assumptions. His employees were going to think he wasn't working. They were going to think he was sick, or something serious was wrong. So I asked him, "What if they're thinking the opposite of that? What if they're thinking, 'Wow, this guy's really successful! He doesn't have to come in all the time. That's the guy I want to work for!'? What if they're thinking, 'Gosh, I wish he'd spend more time out of the office so I could get some work done!'?" (We've all either heard that or said that somewhere along the line, haven't we?)

So, my client eventually turned his thinking around and he realized, "You know, I really do need to be out more, and I will explain my thinking to my staff as to why."

And after he started getting out more and he started seeing more people, guess what? He got more business because he's an awesome guy, and he's somebody that just naturally attracts people. His instincts were good, but he was locked down by his assumptions. And it's surprising how often assumptions will impact a relationship, or any of several things during your day-to-day business. This is true in your work life and your personal life. To me, it's all the same.

So what are some assumptions that you might be making? I assure you, everyone makes assumptions. One common assumption you might be making is, "Oh, you can't find good help anymore."

Well, how do you know if you can't get good help if you don't try? You could try hiring people for values and train them, and actually take the time to show them what to do.

Another assumption people often make is, "I'll never be truly successful." When you say things like that, it might be because you haven't defined what success is to you. Or you might have to get out of your comfort zone to find it.

The "I" in GAILs stands for Interpretations. When you interpret, you develop an opinion. When you develop an opinion, then by default, you're ruling out all other options.

So the interpretation of situations is where you see something happen and you read it. And the simple fact is that you can make the absolute wrong judgment or interpretation of almost any situation. The way you see the situation becomes your truth. There is no doubt that's how you see it, but that might not be really what's happening.

There are many situations where you can interpret something that might not actually be what's happening. And that can impact how you see the world and how you see yourself. There's "true," and then there's "truth." There's what's true for you, which is not necessarily the truth. The goal is to get to the truth of the situation so that you can move past it, learn from it, or capture the opportunity. An incorrect interpretation can cause issues, conflicts, and misunderstandings, as well as lead to missed opportunities.

I once went on a joint call with an advisor. The first thing that the advisor's client brought up was, "What am I getting for my fees?"

Now, when I heard that, I said to myself, "Oh, great start!"

This particular client was paying a lot of money in fees. He had a $4,000,000 account, but the advisor's first response to him was, "Well, we'll just lower your fee."

That was the advisor's reaction because his interpretation of the situation was that the client was literally saying he was paying too much in fees. That was the advisors "true," but the real "truth" was that the advisor wasn't doing a good enough job of demonstrating the value for the fees being paid. So it was a value-recognition issue, not a literal "I'm paying you too much" complaint. The client just wanted to see what he was getting for the fees that he was paying. Pretty simple. But the advisor's interpretation created an entirely different dynamic, which put us into a whole discussion about how we might lower fees and how we might look at cutting costs, and that turned out to be the wrong issue.

And long story short is that this particular client is now gone.

There was a failure to demonstrate the value received for the fees paid. The advisor kept reacting to the initial question, "What am I getting for my money?" The client was saying, in essence, "I'm literally asking you what I'm getting?"

No matter how low the fees went, there still wasn't a recognition of value. So that is an example of where an incorrect interpretation created a bad outcome for the advisor.

The "L" in GAILs, the fourth energy block, represents Limiting beliefs. A limiting belief is where you've either bought into something and this is now your truth, or you've actually convinced yourself about some idea. You have convinced yourself that this is just the way it is. This is something of which you need to be conscious, and understand how this might be holding you back from getting what you want. An example of a limiting belief is, "Successful people are just lucky. I mean, honestly, I work hard, but those people are just lucky. They don't work any harder than I do."

Another example of a limiting belief is, "Life insurance is sold and not bought." (You're likely saying to yourself, "Well, that's true!"). How about, "The earth is flat," or, "The four-minute mile can never be broken!"?

Can you think of some limiting beliefs that you may have that could be holding you back from what you want?

Impostor Syndrome

There is a second set of energy blocks I want to share with you, and this set is called the impostor syndrome. Impostor syndrome (also known as impostor phenomenon, fraud syndrome, or the impostor experience) is a psychological pattern in which a person doubts their accomplishments and has a persistent internalized fear of being publicly exposed as a "fraud." The term was coined by American psychologists Pauline R. Clance and Suzanne A. Imes, who published an article called "The Imposter Phenomenon in High Achieving Women: Dynamics and Therapeutic Intervention" in 1978 in the journal *Psychotherapy Theory, Research & Practice*.

This is something that I know even the top producers in the financial services business experience. Everyone probably has some of level of impostor syndrome. I know I certainly struggled with it during my career

One of its symptoms is procrastination. Do you ever procrastinate? Have you ever wondered why you procrastinate? After all, we're professionals aren't we? Don't we have at least some level of specialized education? Haven't we been in the business for a while? Then why do we procrastinate?

Too often, we get an opportunity, and we just sit there with it. And in my own case, it was always the bigger the opportunity, the longer it sat. I always wondered, why is that? Why am I not acting on this? Why wouldn't I want to just go get that opportunity as fast as possible, make that happen? Some people do. They don't procrastinate. The way I got around it was that I delegated a lot of tasks so that I didn't have to procrastinate, because I found that I was the clog in the pipeline, because of my procrastination.

I finally realized that my procrastination came from my impostor syndrome.

Here's an example of how this showed up with me. In my firm, we created a lot of financial plans. A prospect or client would come in and we would go over what our process looked like, what the benefits were, and what the cost would be to them. If they agreed to hire us, which they usually did, we began gathering data. At this point, I had created the expectation in the prospect's mind as to how wonderful it would be to have their financial life all planned out. And it was true; it is very beneficial to put together a financial plan so that one can make good decisions as one moves toward financial and life goals.

Our process was that we would have this meeting, maybe a second one to make sure we had all the information and the goals were clear, and then we would take all that data and information and create a financial plan document for the prospect to complete with projections and detailed recommendations with action items. This is where the trouble started. You see, while we did get paid a fee to create the plan and the document, we also got paid fees on any money they brought to us for management. We also earned commissions on any financial products. So, there was a lot at stake for me. While I delegated the data organization and input of the information into our software, I was responsible for reviewing the document for accuracy and, most importantly, writing the recommendations and creating the action items.

Because my Gremlin involves being judged, I would be frozen with fear- fear that we had made a mistake in the numbers, fear that I had made an incorrect recommendation, fear that the prospect would be disappointed or that the plan wasn't good enough and therefore I wasn't good enough. And fear that even after all that work to get everything just right, the prospect wouldn't act on any of our recommendations, which would mean no money to manage and no commissions to be earned.

So, the file sat on my desk! That way nothing could go wrong. The only issue there was that my staff would keep asking me, "When will you be done with that file so we can set up a meeting with the client?"

"Soon," I would say. And the file continued to sit and sit—until the pressure built up so much that I finally had to do it and present it. It was an excruciating process for me. Every day I would do everything else I had to do except that one big thing. I would deal with all the low-hanging fruit every day, but that file sat there, looking at me, as if to say, "You're not qualified to be doing this. You don't deserve this. They will pick this apart and buy nothing!"

Eventually, I became more confident and my procrastination diminished. But it was always there at a low level, and I learned to push through it, as I became more self-aware of why I was feeling that way. Eventually, I delegated all parts of the plan creation to others except for the front-end meeting and the plan presentation. I gave up control and managed the process. Guess what? The quality went up, we turned over more plans, and we implemented almost everything we recommended. The key for all the issues was to diminish my role in the process.

Another thing that comes with impostor syndrome is relentless second-guessing. Consider whether you constantly think about too many things at once and second guess yourself:

- "Gosh, I wish I would have done it differently."

- "Why'd I do that?"

- "Maybe I should've done it this way."

- "I was going to do it that way, but now I'm thinking I'm going to do it this way. So I'll just procrastinate a little bit longer until I figure it out."

And wow, this gets to be a real issue! What ends up happening is that you tend to set your goals too low so that you can achieve them in spite of yourself, and you stay in your comfort zone and your fixed mindset. So next time you start second guessing yourself, just step back for a second and ask yourself, "Why am I second-guessing myself here? What am I missing?"

Another symptom of impostor syndrome is a feeling of guilt. Does this resonate with you? Come on, everyone experiences some feelings of guilt. But where's it coming from, and why? What are you feeling guilty about? Is it something that you said to a client or prospect?

Maybe what you told him or her wasn't quite accurate. Or maybe there were some things that you could have disclosed a bit more about a product that you were presenting to them. Maybe you feel guilty about being successful. Are you asking yourself whether you are even allowed to earn this much money?

Sometimes you may feel guilty because you've actually had some success, and you think, "Do I really deserve this? Is it okay for me to earn a commission this large on this transaction?" Or you may say, "Wow, they are paying a lot of fees to my firm. Is that okay?"

These feelings of guilt can create self-sabotage and ultimately can keep you from actually trying because you don't want to experience those uncomfortable feelings.

Another common symptom of impostor syndrome is people pleasing. This is a significant issue for people who sell for a living. People pleasing is part of this whole issue when you're not confident about who you are because of the impostor syndrome. And you will do things for people so they'll approve of you and like you. This is a common issue in our business because we really want people to love us, don't we?

If you're like most advisors, you love your clients, and you like it that they love you so much. And that's a great feeling. For many advisors, that feeling is the reason they're in the business in the first place. That's why a lot of people don't ever leave this industry; they have such a strong need to have clients love them all the time. The issue arises when you have too many clients you shouldn't have just because these clients are more people to love you even though they don't really make money for you.

Another often-seen symptom of the impostor syndrome is fear. Fear will stop you in your tracks if you have the impostor syndrome: "Boy, I've got a chance to do something big here, but I'm just too afraid to do it. I can't do it. I just know I'll fail."

Or there's a fear even worse than the fear of failure. You actually may succeed! Then what?

Every one of us has fear. Advisors don't always fess up to it, but you need to face the fear and act anyway. If you're like most advisors, you are usually never as ready as you feel you need to be, but are rarely as underprepared as you think you are.

If you have experienced any of these feelings or issues, you might have some level of impostor syndrome. And although you might not even be aware of it, it's a huge energy drain on you. When you procrastinate, you feel guilty because you haven't gotten back to people. You don't get back to the people because you're afraid that they're not going to buy anything from you. You don't know if they're going to approve. Or you feel the need to make modifications to your original proposal so you can please them. And as you can see, now you're in a vicious cycle. They might find out who you really are! Or they may learn that you're not as good as they thought you were.

That's all pretty scary stuff!

To further illustrate what I'm talking about, I'm going to debunk a few lies* that you may say to yourself when you have some level of the impostor syndrome:

- "My self-doubt is proof that I'm inadequate." In reality, sometimes self-doubt is just proof that you're human, not inadequate. The fact that you doubt yourself just proves you're a human being. That's a fact. So if you get into a situation where you doubt yourself, remind yourself that you're having those doubts because you're human.

- "Successful people don't have these feelings." Well that's absolutely not true, because many well-known people, such as actress and comedian Tina Fey, suffer from impostor syndrome and have talked about it publicly. You've probably heard of Maya Angelou, the great poet and author. No doubt you've heard of Stephen King, the horror novelist and story writer. These people are among a list of hundreds of famous successful people with impostor syndrome. These are people who are highly successful and who have learned how to manage their impostor syndrome. They've learned to recognize when they start feeling this way. They go to the source and ask themselves, "Why am I feeling this? What's behind these feelings and thoughts?" And then they move forward.

- "I'm not ready. I'd love to do this, but I'm not ready." I always say if that's how you're feeling, go ahead and do it anyway, even if you're not ready. The fact is you're usually ready enough. Yes, you may need more training. Yes, all advisors need continuing education. Do you want to stretch your mind and get better at what you do? Yes. But you're ready enough to show up just as you are.

- "It's just a matter of time before all this success comes crashing down around me." Take an objective look at all the success that you have managed to achieve, and ask yourself whether it's even possible that it all isn't true. Is it even possible that at this point in your career, the other shoe is likely to drop to reveal your lack of success? Not likely.

- "I have nothing useful or original or important to say." Sure, that one's crossed my mind a few times, even when I was preparing for this book. But we all have something to say. Whatever your way is, that's the right way. And when you realize that just you being authentic and showing up in front of your clients for their benefit is enough, that's the right way. And unique is good. I recently heard someone say, "Being unique is better than being better." We live in a world of commoditization. Unfortunately, we advisors tend to all look alike to consumers. Everyone is charging 1% to manage money, everybody has the same life and health insurance products, and everything's becoming levelized. How are you going to differentiate yourself? Unique is good, so be confident and accept that.

- "I can't trust the praise of others." Well, this is where you just have to believe it when someone tells you how awesome you are. People will tell you how good you are simply because they think you're good. And you should go with that and believe it.

- "Asking for help is for losers; it is a sign of weakness." Too many people are afraid to ask for help, so they just sit there and struggle. But the people who care about you really do want you to succeed, so you need to let them help you succeed.

You are so fortunate to work in a business in which the people pride themselves on sharing and mentoring. The members of the Million Dollar Round Table (MDRT) will tell you that is the number one "value add" to membership. Help is everywhere in the financial services business, and the tradition lives on because people who have been helped and mentor almost always become people who help and mentor others themselves.

You are in the right business!

Before Moving On, Ask Yourself…

1. What are three things your Gremlin says to you that you can reframe?

_____
_____
_____
_____

2. What assumptions are you living with that are holding you back?

_____
_____
_____
_____

3. What limiting beliefs are most important for you to challenge if you are to be successful?

_____

_____

_____

_____

* Energy Blocks and GAILs are terms used by IPEC, the Institute of Professional Excellence in Coaching's training program, developed by Bruce D. Schneider. Gremlins, Assumptions, Interpretations and Limiting Beliefs are generic elements widely used in the coaching field without copyright protection but were first introduced to me during my training with IPEC.

* These questions are adapted from, and attributed to, Tanya Geisler, a peer coach who works exclusively with Imposter Syndrome.

CHAPTER 3

Seven Levels of Attitudinal Perspective

"Your attitude, not your aptitude, will determine your altitude."

— Zig Ziglar

So much of how effective you are in your day-to-day life comes from your response or reaction to what happens to you – whether or not you are in control of the situation. As you become more self-aware of this, you will gain the ability to check yourself when in stressful or frustrating situations. Stephen Covey wrote about this in his classic book *The 7 Habits of Highly Effective People*. The ability to choose how to respond versus simply reacting is the core definition of responsibility—"response-ability," the ability to respond. Earlier, I discussed inner blocks in your thinking and the adjustments you can make to open up opportunities, be happier, and be more attractive to people, but now I will introduce you to a new concept focused on your attitude and your perspective. In other words, this concept focuses on how you see the world around you.

How Do You View The World Around You?

When I write or talk about this question, I'm talking about what I have named The 7 Levels of Attitudinal Perspective ™. I have adapted this concept from the 7 Levels of Energy Leadership created by Bruce D. Schneider founder of The Institute of Professional Excellence In Coaching (iPEC).* Bruce introduced the 7 Levels in his book *Energy Leadership*. I adapted the concept to introduce this to financial advisors. These attitudinal levels of perspective are the lenses through which you see the world. This is how you view the world. These levels act as your filters and they affect how you respond to situations. As individuals, we view the world through filters (based on our experiences, values, assumptions, etc.). These filters will either limit what you see (like tunnel vision) or expand what you see (like a prism), and thus, impact how you perceive and what you think about your circumstances. This, in turn, impacts how you show up in different situations. These levels describe how you respond and react, especially to stress and stressful situations. And your energy comes from these seven levels of perception. This attitude or energy either attracts people or repels people.

Think in terms of the law of attraction. For instance, if you show up in any kind of relationship with the perception and attitude of a victim—if you see everything as somebody else's fault—then that's going to put off a certain kind of energy. I am sure you know people like this. We all have people in our lives who are a drain on us. But we also all know people who naturally lift us up. We want to tap into their energy because their attitude literally energizes us!

There are seven energy levels that Bruce identified that I will introduce to you now as attitudinal levels.

Level One of Attitudinal Perception: Level one is the attitude of a victim. The dominant thought of people with this attitude is that the world is happening to them. Everything that happens in their life is happening to them. They are at the mercy of what's happening around and to them. When you see people walking around like this, they have a lethargic kind of attitude and are apathetic. They sometimes feel a lot of guilt. They may have self-doubt. "What's the point?" they ask, because after all, "What can I do about it anyway?"

They tend to be indifferent. And their dominant thought is, "I am going to lose anyway so what's the point of trying?"

Level one is a negative kind of energy. It's what is called catabolic energy.* Catabolic energy is a drain on the person who possesses it, and it's a drain on other people. So when you show up like this and go through life in a catabolic state, people don't want to be around you. Frankly, you don't even want to be around yourself when you're in this level of perspective.

Level Two of Attitudinal Perception: Level two is about conflict and struggle. Sometimes, when you find yourself down at level one and you're feeling at the mercy of life—when everything's happening to you and there's nothing you can do about it—you can get angry. You can generate conflict when you push back and declare, "I'm not going to take it anymore. I'm going to do something about it."

When that happens, you go straight to anger and get into conflict. Your dominant thought becomes, "Well, I'm defiant."

And now, your attitude shifts to thinking, "I'm going to win, and you're going to lose."

A clear example of what I mean is when somebody cuts you off in traffic. Typically, your dominant thought in that situation is not, "Oh, no, after you, please."

No. In most instances like this, your dominant thought will be, "Yeah. I'm a victim here. That guy cut me off and now I'm angry."

Maybe you are even thinking, "I'm going to go and cut him off."

As you can see, attitudes can shift and escalate quickly, and you can get into a reactive mindset when a stressful situation develops.

But after levels one and two, as you get into the higher levels of perspective, you start to get into more of a responsive kind of energy level.

Level Three of Attitudinal Perception: Now consider level three. At level three, you are in what's called anabolic,* or positive, energy. At this level of perspective, you're starting to realize, "Hey, you know what? Some of what's happened to me is my responsibility."

At this level, you're accepting responsibility and being accountable for your way of managing a particular situation. Acceptance is a dominant thought.

In addition, at this level you are looking for ways to compromise and cooperate. Another dominate thought here is, "I want to win, and hopefully you'll win too."

Here you start thinking things like the following:

- "Maybe I could have handled that better."

- "I probably could have thought about that in a different way."

- "So, let's see how we can work this out."

- "I'm still going to win, but hopefully, you'll win too."

Level Four of Attitudinal Perception: Level four is a service mentality where you have concern for others. And in using that traffic incident example from level two, remember that somebody cut you off with his or her car and your immediate response was, "This is happening to me, and I'm angry about it."

But with a level four perspective, all of a sudden you stop and say to yourself, "That person has a higher need to get where they want to go than I do, or they're just a jerk."

Either way, you're letting it go. You're putting *them* before you. If they want to go, let them go. Maybe they're late picking up their kid from daycare or something else just as important, and who are you to get in the way?

So a level four perspective is where you have concern for others, and you are focused on compassion and empathy. The dominant thought here is the other person wins. You see this a lot in the financial services business. In this business, people tend to be service minded; people want to help other people. If you are a parent, you want to put your children before yourself. If you have a good relationship with your partner, you know that you want to help them first. This level of perspective is all about putting other people before you, and the dominant thinking is, "They win. That's all I really care about."

Just for the record, these levels of perspective, or energy levels, fluctuate up and down and all around throughout the day. Some people just seem to always be happy and they're always relaxed, so those people are spending more time in higher levels of energy and attitude. Their perspective is to look at the world and say, "We are going to work it out and it's going to happen," and, "Please, you go first," or "Let me do that for you."

Others are, well, not quite that way. And so you resonate and fluctuate mostly positive all throughout the day, except for when that driver cuts you off. Then it's straight to levels one and two! The question is, how do you get off those levels quickly? That's an important question to address, because if you stay down at those lower levels and frequently perceive the world like that, you are seriously hurting yourself and you're not very pleasant to be around. Then you become that person who walks into a room and everyone's energy is being drained; you're the drainer!

Everyone resonates at a low level sometimes, usually in stressful situations, but the trick is to move off of that. How can you open your mind up and say, "You know what, here's a situation where I can probably work this out so that you can win."

Level Five of Attitudinal Perception: Even better, you can go to level five, which is an attitude about reconciliation. On this level, you're really trying to work things out and with no judgment. You're just happy and at peace and at this level of attitude, you're thinking, "We all win or nobody wins".

At this level, you're really thinking about teamwork. I see this in high-functioning life insurance agencies; everybody's on the same page, with the same message. They're moving forward, and everybody's trying to help everyone else because there's no point in doing what they're doing unless everyone is going to win and benefit from the efforts.

Level Six of Attitudinal Perception: Level six goes into synthesis or intuition. Here, there's a state of joy and an attitude of pure appreciation for where you are and what you're doing. It's a level of wisdom. It's an attitude of "everybody always wins," where you're thinking that as long as you can help everybody move forward in life, then everybody's winning.

Level Seven of Attitudinal Perception: And the final and highest attitudinal level is level seven. The characteristics at this level are non-judgment, absolute passion, and genius thinking. Do you ever have those flashes of brilliance where you thought of something clever or you've said just the right thing in a client meeting? Or things just flow when you're talking to people? Or your relationship's going really, really well? These things are probably happening because your attitude has shifted to one of these higher levels. And what's really cool about all this is that after you know about these levels, you can constantly move yourself up. You have control over how you shift into the higher levels of attitude and perspective. It's all about learning to control your response, and not just react. In short, it is about being responsible.

Here's a true story from my own life that is an example of what I'm talking about. One day a few years ago, my wife and I were playing golf at a nice resort course. This was on a Friday afternoon, a beautiful fall day. We had the golf course almost completely to ourselves. It was just the two of us. It was the best. There was nobody behind us, and nobody in front of us. We were playing fast and pretty well. And we were really enjoying being outside together.

All of a sudden, I drove our golf cart around the bend to the next tee box, and there were eight golf carts sitting there occupied by a bunch of young guys, drinking beer and smoking cigars. Oh, man. What level do you think I went to? I confess. I quickly went down to level one, with this immediate reaction: "Look what's happening to me. Ruining my golf day. My beautiful round of golf is now going down the tubes because of these guys."

And then I got angry very quickly. I'm thinking, "These guys! I'm not putting up with this."

At that point and that quickly, I'm in level two. And I'm determined to do something about the situation. "I'm angry and I'm going to call the pro shop and put a stop to this," I think. "They are wrecking my day. They're not supposed to have all those carts out here."

But then I remembered that I'm a coach and that I've had this training. So I recognized I'm at level two. What's my next level up? Level three. Compromise. What is the situation here? What's the interpretation of the event? I interpreted the event this way: "Oh, you know, it's Friday afternoon, and this resort is famous for weddings. Hmm. I wonder if those guys are in a wedding party having a little bachelor outing. And I'll bet all the girls are back at the hotel getting their hair done and getting ready for the big rehearsal dinner. And here are these guys having so much fun out here. They're young guys, and they're just having an awesome day."

I realized at that point that there were only four more holes to play. And I started thinking, "Gosh, what am I? A grumpy old man? Am I really going to call the pro shop and just break up their good time?"

That sure didn't seem right. So then I moved up one more level to level four, where I started thinking, "Let's let them take their time."

I told my wife, "We've got beer in the cooler. Let's just relax for a little bit."

We opened a beer, and we sat there together. We waited about ten minutes. Eventually, the group of guys moved on up ahead. It was awesome. I shifted my attitudinal perspective and my energy to a place where I could be happy. They could have what they needed. I just recognized that they were only having fun. It was a big weekend for them. And watching them, I remembered all the times that I had done something similar when I was younger and at that stage of my life.

So that's just a quick example of how you can shift your energy, how you can stop and reinterpret a situation, how you can jump off of assumptions and move forward.

I have been using examples of general life situations, but now I will share an example of how this worked for me in a business situation. There were times when things weren't going well for me in my business. Cash flow was less than great, I was having staff issues, and the prospect list wasn't that great either. I had debt and overhead. So the pressure was on.

When I was in that situation it was very easy for me to live in a level one and level two world. These things were happening *to* me, and I was the victim of all this bad luck! "Where are all the prospects?" I asked.

"Why can't my employees think for themselves? When will I ever get out from under this pressure?"

It's easy to spiral down like this, and I suspect it happens to everyone from time to time. Back when this happened, though, I wasn't aware of these attitudinal perspectives and the concept of shifting my perspective.

But I knew enough to realize that it was all on me and that nothing was going to change unless I took responsibility and made some changes. That's a level three mindset. One day when I was feeling down, I decided to do something that wouldn't solve any of my problems, but might just make me feel better. Late in the afternoon, after sitting at my desk and waiting for something to happen, I decided to pick up the telephone and call one of my recently widowed clients. I just called to see how she was doing. It made her day. And it turned me around.

She spent the whole call talking about how much I had helped her and how she couldn't have gotten through it without me. And then I totally forgot how bad things were, because compared to her challenges mine were minor. After I got off the telephone, I remembered how important the things I do for people are, and it renewed my sense of purpose.

Unknowingly, I shifted to level four by making that telephone call. And now I was actually excited and motivated to deal with my challenges. I started calling people again and guess what? I started getting meetings, and meetings led to sales. And sales led to cash flow, debt reduction, and hiring additional staff.

Now, this didn't happen overnight, but that one shift in my mindset turned the tide and set me on a path toward success. I got back to levels five and six, where I saw opportunity everywhere, and I reconnected with my higher purpose as an advisor (level seven.) The key was at level four, where I put someone else's needs before my own. I had no idea when I picked up that telephone that this would happen, but it did. That's what is so cool about it. I wasn't looking for any particular outcome. I was just trying to help someone else that day. And it renewed my spirit.

In the end, I really believe that there's not much difference between general life and business when it comes to gaining perspective and shifting you energy and your attitude. After all, it's still you in both environments. If you can get to a place with your clients where you can open up and be vulnerable to people and let them know who you really are, you will attract a lot of people who want to be near you.

Now let's get back to level seven. You can't live at level seven, because that's for someone like the Dalai Lama. Assuming you're not the Dalai Lama or someone like him, then you are a little bit more high maintenance. Level seven, however, is something that you will experience from time to time, and you can recognize it when you have these moments. Sometimes they come in a group situation. Sometimes they happen in creative environments. You will recognize level seven, because you will have this kind of experience where everything's just going just absolutely great. Believe me, people will *want* to be near you when you are operating on level seven.

One example I can relate to is the MDRT Annual meeting. At those meetings, all of the MDRT producers are there feeding off of one another's high-level energy, and it is practically nirvana to experience it. There no one is thinking at all about winning or losing. Truly, these meetings represent the level-seven experience.

The takeaway here is simply this: You get to choose. You get to choose how you show up in the world. You get to choose how you *respond* versus *react* to situations that aren't going your way. You can choose with which level of attitudinal perspective you view the world.

You can learn to recognize what level you are currently in and shift to a higher level. You can choose to be kind or you can choose to be mean. You can choose to be a victim, or you can choose to be a creator. You can choose to be happy or you can choose to be miserable. It's all up to you. You do have 100% control over this!

So, choose responsibly! Strive to become "response-able."

Before Moving On, Ask Yourself...

1. When thinking of the seven levels, to which levels do you tend to go when you're in stressful situations?

_____

_____

_____

_____

2. When not stressed, what level are you in when you are feeling most happy and productive?

_____

_____

_____

_____

3. How "response-able" are you in terms of shifting your energy levels from low to high?

_____
_____
_____
_____

* *This chapter contains my interpretation of the copyrighted work of Bruce D. Schneider and the Institute for Professional Excellence in Coaching (iPEC). The terms catabolic and anabolic and the descriptions of the seven levels are attributed to Bruce D. Schneider and iPEC. Used with permission from Bruce D. Schneider founder of The Institute of Professional Excellence in Coaching (iPEC).*

CHAPTER 4

Six Mindsets of Success

"You must learn a new way to think before you can master a new way to be."
                              - Marianne Williamson

Even a small shift in your thinking can have a huge impact on the trajectory of your future and a big influence on your success. Your mindsets are your truths based on your values as well as your experiences in life. As with limiting beliefs, you buy into this thinking and you believe it, in some cases, to your detriment because it closes out other possibilities. Controlling your mindset is key to having the things that you want in life. So let me introduce you to six mindsets of success that may be instrumental to unlocking your thinking and freeing you up to make big changes in your life. If you can change your mindset, you can change your future!

Changing Your Mindset Can Change Your Future

In previous chapters I've written about how you see yourself and how you view the world. Now I'm going to address the importance of how you think and how the way you are thinking can be holding you back from getting what you want. As you read through these six mindsets, try to recall situations where these concepts have appeared in your life and how they may have affected you.

Mindset Number One: In this mindset, you place way too much importance on making other people feel good.

Let me just put it out there—it is very important for you stop trying so hard to please other people. This is a real issue that is prevalent in our society. Based on what you see on social media, television, and in the movies, you would believe that we're in a self-gratification environment. But a lot of what we do when we interact with others we do primarily because we want to avoid conflict or receive validation from other people. I'm not talking about customer service. I'm talking about sacrificing your own values and subordinating your own needs and violating your own boundaries in matters that involve what you will accept and what you won't accept.

And this is especially true with your prospects and clients. You're busy trying to run a business. You will do whatever it takes, including running appointments at seven or eight o'clock at night—or even on weekends. I wonder, what's the "why" behind that? Is it because you don't want to tell your prospect or client that you're open from 9:00 a.m. to 6:00 p.m., so you can meet with him within those hours? Is it because you're afraid your prospect or client will be unhappy with you if you don't accommodate him or her? Is it because you want to please him, especially because he already is a client and you want to show him that you'll do whatever you have to do to keep his business, even if it means not being home for dinner or skipping the gym when you committed to yourself to get in shape?

There are many reasons why you might want to please people like that. But here's the challenge. You talk to a lot of people who aren't helping you or your business when you're in people-pleasing mode, especially when you're prospecting, and you keep a lot of clients who aren't the right clients as well.

You do this, and you let them run you ragged creating overwhelming "busyness." Then you try to segment your book of business. But you're incapable of segmenting your book of business because that would mean providing different levels of service to different people, and in people-pleasing mode you just want to "love" all your clients the same. You say, "It's just easier to do the same thing for everybody."

So you can't segment your book of business because you might not please some clients. Ultimately, that means everybody gets your newsletter, and everyone gets a discounted fee. Everybody gets four meetings a year—or six meetings a year—and all of a sudden you have a business that is controlling you instead of the other way around.

You also give up a lot of profit when you run your business this way, because when you're not segmenting your book of business, you're naturally losing profit. That's because you're providing the same level of service for people who don't generate the same levels of revenue. So when you have a higher-revenue client, you can afford to give them a higher level of service, which is what they're paying for and what they typically require. But you don't have to provide that same level of service to somebody who bought an insurance policy from you ten years ago. But yet you do.

And so your life becomes all-around people pleasing, and it causes you to be incredibly inefficient. When you operate like this, it's hard to create a process. You end up with a hundred "one offs" in your practice, so everyone gets a little bit different service so you can keep them happy. "Well," you end up saying to yourself, "he likes his spreadsheet this way, and she likes it that way, and he likes to come in on Tuesday night, and she likes to come in on Saturday morning."

All of a sudden, you're just running all over the place. That's not really a good business model. Certainly not one I would want.

So how does this sound as an alternative? You have a business where you have defined hours, you have a defined target market, and you can build a process around all the things that need to be done. Then you can delegate tasks, you can automate processes, you can outsource some functions, and you can become very efficient. Then you can provide the appropriate level of service to the appropriate clients, so that you actually can make profit. Doesn't that sound better? You can also have a life. You can be home for dinner with your children, if that's important to you, or you can take time to exercise.

So why isn't that the alternative you're using?

I'm not standing in judgment. I know that early in an advisor's career you have to be a bit less selective in order to build your client base. But that's not a sustainable model. I'm just saying there could be a better way, and suggesting that you find out what's behind your behavior. If the only reason you're overly accommodating is just because you don't want to get the rejection or reaction from your clients and you don't want to risk them leaving, then that's not really a good reason. I want you to examine why you're doing what you're doing and consider a shift of your mindset around this issue.

Mindset Number Two: The second mindset, for me, is perhaps the most important one, and it has to do with differentiating oneself from the rest of your competitors.

We live in a world of sameness, especially in the insurance and financial services business, and what really got me thinking about this was when the industry was facing the Department of Labor (DOL) fiduciary rule in the United States. Even outside of the United States, everybody's pretty much charging the same fees, has the same disclosures, and the marketplace has become super flat. So how do you differentiate yourself from other people? How would you answer if someone asked you, "Why should I do business with you when I can do business with her just as easily and for the same price?"

How would you answer that? What's your value proposition? You have to be completely clear about how you provide value. I think it is so important that you're able to articulate artfully your value to your clients. You've likely heard it before, that the value is you or the value proposition is Feature X or Feature Y. The story I wrote about earlier regarding the advisor who lost the client because that client didn't recognize the advisor's value is a good example of the issue I'm talking about. Indeed, that advisor didn't do a good enough job of articulating his value to his client.

A good way to work out your value proposition and value statement is to ask yourself the following questions:

- "Who am I?"

- "What am I known for?"

- "What problems do I solve?"

- "What makes me different?"

- "What gets me excited?"

- "What makes me an expert?"

- "What's unique about me?"

- "What do I believe?"

If you can go through and truthfully answer these questions, I think you will find it very helpful. I recommend that you spend some quality time on this.

I'll share with you what my value proposition was when I was an advisor. I developed this when I was in the coaching program. My value proposition was simple. It was: "Our firm provides value through leadership, relationship, and creativity."

The leadership portion is where we provided direction for our clients. And we provided perspective about what was really happening and why it was happening.

The relationship portion was all about integrity and trust. This is where our clients came to know instinctively and through our demonstrations of how we worked with them that we always put them and their interests first. They knew we would put their needs before ours. They knew our values. The relationship portion was very foundational in that sense, which is why we put that as a high priority in our value proposition.

The third portion was creativity because the creativity enabled us to help our clients maximize whatever opportunities they may have had. We took a 360-degree view of their situation. We didn't just come out with the television mass-marketing financial guru method of "this is how you have to do it" or some similar "one size fits all" mass-marketing boiler plate method. We even challenged conventional thinking on occasion. We would look around their challenges and think outside of the box and say, "There may be a better way for you."

We didn't always advise clients to pay off mortgages. We didn't always suggest that clients put a whole lot of money down on a house. We didn't always encourage clients to invest in bonds exclusively in their retirement plans. There might be different reasons to do different things, so we would walk around that issue until we found a suitable solution. So "leadership, relationship, and creativity" was how we communicated our value proposition to our clients and prospects.

The other part of the discussion regarding our value was where we talked with clients about things we can control and things we can't control. This is especially important in the investment arena. I would always tell clients, "There are five things we talk about in investments. Four we can control and one we can't. We can control taxes to some degree, and use strategies to minimize taxation. We can manage to that. We can control costs by choosing low-cost providers in various platforms and products. We can control risk through asset allocation, diversification, and insurance. And we can control—or at least influence—behavior. If we can influence your behavior, we can help you make good decisions and avoid bad decisions. If we can do this, especially in markets that become volatile, then we can have a better outcome. So those are the four things we can control: taxes, costs, risk, and behavior. The one thing we can't control is performance, because we don't control the Fed, we don't control who's president, and we don't control Brexit. We don't control China. We don't control the stock market."

So ask yourself this, why in the world would somebody put himself or herself out there, and sit down four or more times a year with somebody, and talk about performance? I have never understood it. Yes, you will have to address performance, but you will want to come at it from the highest altitude prospective. You will want to elevate the conversation and bring to bear your accumulated wisdom on the matter and redirect the conversation back to their highest-level goals.

Ah, but you likely won't get into that wisdom conversation because of the impostor complex or because of the other blocks and insecurities that you may have that won't enable you to accept that you have wisdom, that you are in fact wise. Even if you're not long in the tooth like I am, you can still have wisdom because of your unique personal experiences. Avoid like the plague talking about price, product, or performance. Those are commodities, and they have very little value in the grand scheme. People ask us about them all the time because that's the only thing they know to ask us.

We have to take a leadership position around this whole value proposition. And we have to be the ones to come in there and ask clients about what's most important to them:

- "What's your why?"

- "Why are you working so hard?"

- "Why are you working 80 hours a week in your company?"

- "Where are you going with this financial plan?"

- "What's your life plan or vision?"

- "What do you want in the end?"

As an advisor, you are an asker of questions, a discoverer of dreams!

You elevate yourself by taking a high-altitude view of your client's situation. When you can get up at 30,000 feet in your thinking and you begin to see how things look from that view, it's tremendously valuable to your clients. Not many people are talking to clients about this. Too many advisors are too busy selling their performance, their products, and their products' features.

I suggest you always try to bring clients up there with you at 30,000 feet and begin talking with them about their why. And as soon as you know a client's why, you'll know your why. It's just that simple. This is very important because when everyone is charging 1% and everyone offers all the same products, you need to be able to differentiate yourself from everyone else. And the way you differentiate yourself is by understanding what you truly have to offer a person that's unique and valuable to them, and being able to artfully communicate this to your client so that they recognize your unique value.

Decades ago before I started in the coaching program, I would take what seemed like a pound of third-party materials with me to every client meeting. Why? I approached meetings this way because I didn't have much confidence. I thought I would impress people because I had all this backup material.

Remember the story about me sending my clients a survey in which I asked them what they thought was my unique value to them? And how about 90% of them wrote back one word or one phrase? They wrote back saying things like, "I knew within five seconds that I could trust you," and, "The minute I met you I could trust you."

Words cannot adequately express what that did for me and my confidence. What it did was make me realize that all I had to do was show up and be me. That was good enough. Yes, I had to do the work. And I did the work. But I didn't have to try so hard up front. In fact, I came to learn that it was off-putting to people when I came in with all that stuff. So I highly recommend that you take some of your clients out to lunch and ask them some high-altitude questions if you want to build deeper long-term relationships.

If you're new in the business, go to some people with whom you have real rapport and ask them these questions. And tell him or her that you're looking to have a long-term relationship and you want to build it on a good foundation. You want to make sure that you're providing value to him or her. And even if you've been around for a long time I think it's a tremendously valuable and important move to go back and have these meaningful encounters with your existing clients.

Mindset Number Three: Accept that failing gracefully is the secret sauce of success. You literally can't succeed if you don't fail. So let's connect back to the question of who we are and what we want. Why aren't we going after it? Why can't we talk back to our Gremlin? And why do we procrastinate? The answer to all of these questions is that we're afraid we're going to fail. And this fear keeps us from even trying.

But the more you fail, the closer you are to succeeding. So it's best to just acknowledge that you know that you're going to fail and you're going to fail often. If you're a baseball fan, you know that the greatest hitters in the history of baseball only hit around .350. That's not even succeeding four out of ten times! So why should you be any different? Why are you expecting to bat 1.000? You're not!

Just get used to the fact there are going to be some strikeouts as you move toward success. That's why I put the term "gracefully" into that mindset. Don't turn your life upside down because something you wanted to happen doesn't happen. Just learn to accept it and move on. Seek out people who believe what you believe and who recognize your value to them. Some will match up, and some will not. That's a fact of life in the advisor's world. Learn to fail gracefully and move on to the next thing, because that means you're getting closer to what you really want.

Mindset Number Four: Be prepared to walk away from the wrong prospects to save space and time in your life for the right ones. There's a practical limit to how many people you can take on as clients, properly service, and provide with what they really need. Of course, if you're building your business, you always can increase your capacity by hiring additional advisors. You also can multiply your capacity through skillful delegation, outsourcing, and automation—all of those things that you do in your practice to build yourself more capacity.

But practically speaking, you only need so many clients if they're the right clients. Then you can build systems around the kind of business you have in place. And the more you focus—the more you hone in on what you really want, who you really want to work with, and what your true value to them is—the more successful you will be.

Your goal is to be authentic and work only with those people with whom you really want to work and those who will accept you as you are and see your value. Then you can just show up as the real you, and build your processes around the relationships you are establishing and build your systems to continue to support that goal. If you can do that, then you're going to build a business that can provide value for you and your family.

As you prospect and build your business, try to replicate your top ten clients, or maybe your top 25. This is not a new approach, and you may well have heard this suggestion before. But that's the principle to follow.

I remember one time many years ago when I analyzed my book of business, and if I remember the numbers correctly, the bottom 45% of my clients were generating only about 5% of my revenue. I loved those people, because I'm a people-pleaser, and they loved me. And everything was good until I realized how it was costing me so much money and profit to have them as clients.

So I thoughtfully and carefully reassigned them to the more appropriate level of service. I assigned some directly with the home office. I assigned some directly with the investment company. I assigned some to other advisors who were looking to start their businesses and who maybe hadn't specialized yet. I didn't just cut them off and fire them. I gave them a new home!

After that process, all of a sudden I was working with the right kind of people, and fewer clients were generating most of my revenue. I then could build business systems around that. Everything felt in sync and everyone was on the same page. Spending less time with the wrong prospects ultimately will lead to you having a clientele filled with the right clients—the kind of clients you want and the kind of clients who will refer you to other people just like themselves.

Mindset Number Five: There is no end point to success, only incremental steps forward. After you define success for yourself, you have to accept that your idea of success is not a destination. Success is not a place you reach. Success is always a moving target, and so you will want to celebrate the little accomplishments that you achieve along the way, as you move toward this ever-changing, ever-rolling target.

Success is an ideal. And because of that, there's no such thing as perfection, only progress. I learned this from The Strategic Coach program when I was a participant decades ago, and it left an impression on me.

I have been thinking about this idea of success having no end point in the context of the GAILs and the Impostor Complex, and I believe at one point I was victim of not properly understanding this. For me and, I believe, many others, perfection is a major cause of procrastination. This happens because you want so badly for something to be perfect, and unless it's perfect, you just don't do it. Or you just put it off until it's perfect, but it'll never be perfect, because there's no such thing as perfection.

And by the way that's the truth in business, and it's the truth in people. No one is perfect. You know that. People say that all the time, but for some reason in business, we expect perfection. I'm not talking about accuracy. Obviously, you don't want to be inaccurate or incorrect, but perfection is this other thing all together. Too many people tend to focus on the perfect world, the perfect scenario, and say things to themselves like, "When things get lined up perfectly, then I'll be happy, and then I'll be successful."

Wrong! That's just never going to happen, because your idea of success is just going to keep rolling, and rolling, and rolling.

Mindset Number Six: Relentlessly pursue the release of control. I heard this idea years ago from the main stage of a National Association of Insurance and Financial Advisors (NAIFA) national conference. MDRT Past President Reggie Rabjohns made this statement, and it really stuck with me.

What does it mean? Relentlessly pursue the release of control. Well, if you think about it, control is really just a form of power. Now I'm not talking about the kind of control where the husband holds the remote control of the TV, and then the wife and kids can never touch it. That's a joke. But seriously, giving up control means giving up power, and it means delegating authority to people. Think about how many people you know—maybe you do this yourself – who have to touch everything in his or her business. When you give up control, you pass control to someone else. You are literally empowering others. When you give control to other people, then you are empowering those people.

It's very impactful when you give up control in all areas of our life, but for now, let's think of it in terms of your business. Think about whether this sounds familiar to you – you are afraid to delegate because "only I can do it right" or because "somebody might mess it up, and if so, then there's a problem, and now I will have to fix it."

But secretly you love fixing things, because you're a good fixer, and that's your real job. And that's what you're good at, so you can put out some more fires tomorrow. Right. Or maybe you say, "I'm so busy that I can't get home, and somehow my day went by, and now I have a late appointment on Tuesday, and oh, my God!"

It becomes this whole vicious cycle. And a lot of it comes from just trying to control everything.

I'm just trying to raise your awareness on this. If you can look for areas in your life where you can release some control and help empower other people, I think you will find some space for yourself to actually focus on what's most important in your life.

As I told one of my coaching clients, it's really very simple. You think your job is to meet with clients and do their financial plans or sales proposals and react to their questions. But that is only *part* of your job. If you have your own business, your job is to make that business profitable. That's number one. Why else would you be working so hard? And to do that, you also have to recognize that your primary responsibility is to run the business.

So far I haven't mentioned anything about meeting with clients. So since you only have so many hours in the day, and you have so many other functions that need to be performed, you will have to make some choices. What do you actually want to do other than the two primary functions I mentioned? Sell? Do the research? Do the proposals? Okay then, you will have to give up everything else and either delegate it to someone or outsource it or automate it. Because that is the only way that you will become profitable, and also the only way that you will be able to achieve some work-life balance.

Most advisors have many of the same skills. Typically, you have awesome social skills, you're intelligent, you have experience, and you're well-educated. If you can just focus on going out and applying your people skills, remembering your education, trusting your experience, and freely exhibiting your knowledge and your wisdom, that would be very powerful! And if you can just bring that powerful package to bear upon people who trust you, then you will become a very influential person, because influence is what fills the void when you give away the power. Give away your power and you become influential. Delegate the power and control to other people, manage them and the process, and you will become more influential.

I think being an influential person is a better role to play than being a controlling person. You can get more done, and it's of much better quality. And that's very meaningful and valuable. And if you can do that with your staff, then you'll become an influential leader in your organization and in in your community.

Focus on that. You don't have to be in charge of everything. Relentlessly pursue the release of control and get your life back.

Remember, I am talking about mindsets here. Just make a small, single-degree change in your trajectory, and it will have a huge impact later on in your life. I encourage you to back through this chapter, and rethink some of these issues, how each one currently impacts your business, and where the challenges of not having these mindsets might be showing up in your life. If you'll do this with an open mind, you just might get closer to success—*your* idea of success.

Before Moving On, Ask Yourself...

1. Which mindsets are draining your energy away from your goals?

   _____
   _____
   _____
   _____

2. Where are your current mindsets limiting your potential for success and happiness?

   _____
   _____
   _____
   _____

3. Which mindsets can you change now that might create a much better outcome?

   _____
   _____
   _____
   _____

CHAPTER 5

Shifting Your Mindset to the High Altitude View

"Change the way you look at things, and the things you look at will change."
— Walter Dyer

Years ago, as I was flying across the United States at 30,000 feet, sitting in my comfy window seat, I became fascinated by the view below. As we flew over small towns, mountain ranges, canyons, and rivers, I noticed that I was getting a completely different, new perspective on the size and scale of the world below. I could see a lot, and I could see far! The gigantic geographical territory below, normally too large to comprehend, was coming into clear view, and I was seeing things in a way I'd never seen them before. I wondered, how could I connect this "high altitude view" to my "ground level" day-to-day life?

When flying over the landscape below, I saw landmarks such as the Grand Canyon and the Great Lakes, but I also could see how the various highways and small roads all came together to form cities, towns, and communities of all sizes. Obviously, the reason I was able to see so much is because I was at such a high altitude. That perspective started to give me a truer sense of the big picture.

Sometime later I started to think more deeply about this in terms of my business. I realized that my business wasn't always just about me sitting across from a client, trying to help him or her solve a problem or fill a particular need. What I was doing in my business was actually a lot more involved than that.

After I started to regularly take this "high altitude view" of my business, I began to see more clearly what was really important in my business life. And what was most important was to try to help my clients achieve the things in their lives that they most wanted to accomplish. It is simple really; if I am able to do that, then I know I can accomplish everything that I need to accomplish.

The great motivational speaker Zig Ziglar famously said, "You can have all the things in life that you want if you will just help enough other people get the things that they want." This way of thinking helps me continually focus on the big picture. By taking the highest altitude view in every situation—not just within my business but also, perhaps more importantly, outside my business – I have improved both my relationships and my results.

In my view, when you are mentally "standing at ground level," you can only see the things that are right in front of you. And even when you turn around, you still have only limited vision from that viewpoint. As you mentally take yourself to the "rooftop," you can see more and can better understand and start to discern patterns and flow. As you go even higher in your thinking, for example in a "tower' or an "airplane," you begin to see things come into focus in a different and much clearer, sharper way. Things start to make more sense from that high altitude perspective.

As I've progressed through my career and my life in general, I've tried to adopt the highest altitude view possible. This view helps me reach beyond my own limiting beliefs and assumptions. It helps me become less judgmental and enables me to broaden my horizons. And ultimately that makes me better able to serve others and help them accomplish what is truly important to them in their own lives.

What does your view look like from "above?"

So many advisors communicate with their clients almost exclusively at "ground level." That is to say, they focus so hard on what is right in front of them and react to client questions about price and performance that they forget to address the big picture with their clients. Of course, there are times when getting into the details is appropriate, but generally speaking advisors and clients would be better served if the advisor focused on the highest-level goals of the clients first and then addressed the "ground level" questions from a high altitude perspective.

By learning to elevate what you focus on during client conversations, you and your clients will reap significant benefits. Clients almost always lead with what is currently on their minds—their "stated" needs—but then quickly move to asking questions about price, product features, and performance. That's because people are conditioned to think that is what they are *supposed* to ask: "What are the costs? How has the performance been? Are there cheaper products out there?"

Think about the questions you ask when in a similar situation, when you are the amateur buyer going up against a full-time professional salesperson. You ask what you think you are supposed to ask so that you'll feel good about being sold or buying something. Everyone does it. It's a defense mechanism based on the reality that most people don't take the time to do the research, or don't have the skill, interest, or inclination to really study the product or service they are seeking. So to protect themselves, people ask the questions that seem most obvious, which are in fact the questions that most advisors dread.

This is often where the advisor misses the opportunity to shift the conversation and get back to the client's original stated "want." What usually happens is that the advisor immediately reacts to the questions and continues to stay down at "ground level," in the weeds with the client. This is not where you want to be; things can spiral badly out of control from there.

This is because often times you end up discussing things over which you have no control, such as performance. This is also the spot in the interaction where inaccurate assumptions and interpretations frequently occur. This often means misunderstandings arise and opportunities are missed.

But here is where you can really create value by bringing perspective to bear and by putting things in proper context for your client. This is especially important when you are discussing issues that are beyond your or your client's control. Frankly, I think this is the most important aspect of your role as an advisor.

Let me give you an example of what I mean. When a client would come into my office with concerns around world events or economic news, for instance, something like BREXIT, the event where the United Kingdom voted to leave the European Union, I would ask them a question. "What about that worries you?"

My question would cause them to take pause and develop an answer. Occasionally, a client would be knowledgeable enough on the subject to actually relate that event to his or her own situation. But usually, the client came in with the concerns based on what he or she saw on television or heard someone else talking about at work. The thinking was, "Well, I guess this is something I should be worried about too!"

At this point, my job was to bring perspective by putting things in context and trying to right size their response. I typically would say, "I certainly understand why that would be something that may cause you to be worried. And it's normal for you to feel that way. But to start with, nothing has been decided yet for sure, and it's actually too early to really know how that could affect you and your situation. But let's go through the possibilities and see whether you really should be concerned or if you will be okay regardless of how it turns out."

Then I would go through and discuss possible impacts, protections we have in place already or that we could put in place, and most importantly, remind the client of the fact that we always will face events over which we have no control. That is why we diversify, rebalance, and review often. Clients sometimes react without all the facts, and your job is to lead them by example and to teach them how to learn to respond.

By developing the skills to suspend that initial client interaction and to stop and focus on the big picture, you enable yourself to gain control over the meeting and focus on the client's highest-level goals. *You* need to be the one asking the questions, and they must be questions about what's most important to the client. What are his or her goals, needs, and dreams? When you pivot to a higher-level conversation, it brings into focus what your client's true underlying desires and goals are. From this higher level of perspective, you can discuss his or her situation in the context of how the client will feel when he or she achieves the goal, fulfills the need, and accomplishes the dream. When you talk with a client at this level, the price, product, data, and additional support information, while sometimes important, take on a smaller, more appropriate role in the decision-making process. When you adopt the High Altitude View, you connect with your clients at a much deeper level; you connect with them around their why. When you know the client's why, you then can be clear about your own why.

So how do you go about adopting the High Altitude View? Let's say a client comes in for a review at a time when the markets are volatile and the client's portfolio is down. The client may very well be scared, nervous, upset, and even angry about the performance of their portfolio. And who wouldn't be, especially if you had recently retired, were facing financial challenges, or were living on a tight budget and dependent on your portfolio's performance?

And let's face it, the media creates a lot of anxiety for your clients. Notice, if you haven't already, how the media – print, television, and online—handles even a modest decline: "Dow Jones Average plummets 100 points today!" Even though a drop like that may represent only a tenth of a percentage point decline, most of your clients will only hear one word: PLUMMETS!

The adage in the news business is, "If it bleeds, it leads." That's why you will never hear someone on the nightly news explain calmly, "The Dow Jones Average moved very little today. In fact, it changed only a tenth of one percent. So don't worry at all about your portfolio." No, that's not their job.

But it *is* your job. Your job is to constantly, consistently and calmly bring perspective to your client's concerns. Your job is to listen to your clients, acknowledge their feelings, and then validate those feelings. Your job is to recognize their questions for what they are and not react, but rather to respond by guiding your clients to take the highest altitude view of the situation.

For example, here's a high altitude response to portfolio concerns: "Mr. and Mrs. Client, I know that you are greatly concerned about your portfolio. It's natural to feel that way, especially given that you have just retired. And I know that when you turn on the news, all you hear is gloom and doom. And that's scary for anyone. The fact is that there are some challenges in the markets currently, so let's take a few minutes to address those and understand how they may be affecting your portfolio."

Mind you, this is not the time for you to become defensive. It's the time to step into a leadership role and calmly explain what is happening, provide unbiased perspective, and give your client clear direction. After you have explained the current financial environment and the causes of the issue, then you can further elevate the conversation: "Let's take a few minutes now to review why we arranged your portfolio in the way that we did. If you will remember, when we constructed your financial plan we discussed your risk tolerance and took into consideration that you would be uncomfortable if the portfolio fluctuated outside of a particular range. Currently, you are still well within that range. The whole point of this is so that you can stay in the portfolio and still be able to sleep at night when things get rocky. Also, when we projected your plan into the future, we assumed a much lower average return that you will likely get long term, so as to take into account the occasional bad stretch like we are currently experiencing in today's markets. And finally, don't forget that we set aside a large amount of cash as a backstop, should we need to make adjustments along the way. So you can feel confident that you are still on track with your goal to retire and enjoy life without worrying about money."

Notice what happens when you speak to a client like this. First, you make the client feel normal. It is normal to feel scared, worried, and upset. Then you explain the reality of what it is that is causing the concerning issue. "Just the facts, Ma'am!" No hype, drama, or defensive behavior. Then you take your client couple back to the original design and remind them why you, *together*, did what you did and how they are still on track, despite the temporary setback. Finally, you reassure them that they will be all right. You provide leadership by giving them perspective and direction, and you take them back to their high-level goal.

This is the way to use the High Altitude View to bring perspective to a situation. Not once is there mention of blame, politics, numbers, comparisons, or the undoing of any plans. You simply restate their goal, remind them of what is important, discuss the things you can control, reassure them, and educate them. In most cases, the client will leave your office feeling much better about their situation, reminded of how smart they were to plan for this eventuality in the first place. They also will see you again as the calm, cool head that they hired in the first place.

By elevating the conversation to the highest altitude view, you enable your client to see everything that is happening and how it all works together. It also right sizes problems, because big things can be seen in relation to other big things and the smallest things almost disappear from sight.

When you operate like this, with the High Altitude View as your mindset, you are bringing to bear your wisdom. You may be thinking to yourself, "Wisdom? I'm too young to have wisdom."

Well, let's address that. What is wisdom exactly?

Merriam-Webster's Dictionary defines wisdom in this way:

1a: ability to discern inner qualities and relationships:

INSIGHT

b: good sense: JUDGMENT

c: generally accepted belief: ". . . challenges what has become

accepted *wisdom* among many historians."

— Robert Darnton

d: accumulated philosophical or scientific learning:

KNOWLEDGE

2: a wise attitude, belief, or course of action

3: the teachings of the ancient wise men (which, I might add,

you and I can access)

When I read this definition, I don't see it mentioned anywhere that one must be old or have a minimum level of experience. I just see that someone must possess the qualities, beliefs, and characteristics that make up wisdom.

Sometimes my staff would tease me that I didn't really do anything in my business. All they would see would be me going into a meeting and hearing laughter or, in some cases, crying, or deliberate discussion from outside the door. They used to ask me, "What do you do in there?" I somewhat jokingly replied, "I just sit down with people and drop wisdom!"

Sure, we conducted the serious review and planning work, but the most valuable aspect of the business was the relationship. And my role in the relationship was to provide wisdom.

Clients and prospects can obtain data, information, and knowledge from almost anyone, anywhere, including the Internet. Those items are commodities. Price, product, and performance... they are all commodities. Commodities have relatively little value in the grand scheme, especially compared to wisdom. I believe it is important to become a Wisdom Based Advisor ™. A Wisdom Based Advisor understands that wisdom is rare in the marketplace, and yet wisdom is the thing most sought after by your prospects and clients.

During my career as a financial advisor, I saw too many of my fellow advisors fail to reach their potential because they focused too much on product, price, and performance. These elements are commodities and as such carry only a minimal and fleeting value.

During the financial crisis of 2008, those of my peers who chose to "get in the weeds" with their clients spent hours upon hours discussing what would happen and what could happen, neither of which was knowable. They were in constant reactive mode and were always on the defense. They were working twice as many hours while their revenue was cut 25% to 45%. That is not a way to survive in business.

And that doesn't even take into account the psychological toll it took. The saying goes, "Live by the sword, die by the sword." They sold performance and took credit when performance was good. And then they had to take credit when performance was bad. It wasn't pretty. Several didn't make it through that crisis and are no longer in the business.

It is critical to first connect with your clients in a deeper, more meaningful way. Establish a relationship based on rapport and trust, and get out of the price and performance conversation. Get people talking about what they want to achieve. Lead them to gain clarity about their goals and dreams.

One tool that is effective in changing that conversation is the Values Pyramid, which is illustrated below. (This pyramid is sometimes called the DIKW pyramid. Its origins are uncertain, but it is commonly used to illustrate the relationships among data, information, knowledge, and wisdom.) I have presented this concept in many speeches and presentations, and people love its simplicity. Often, it's their biggest takeaway.

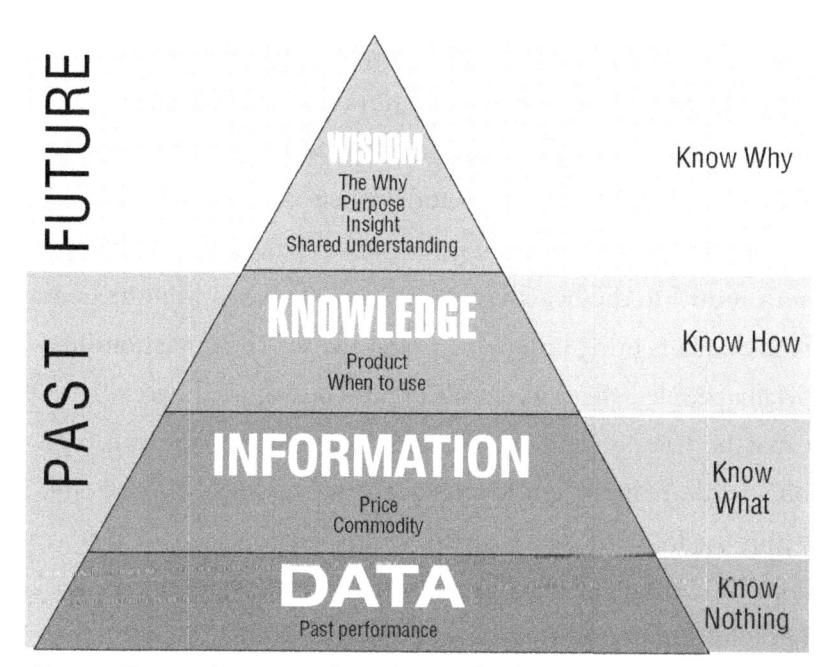

```
FUTURE
         WISDOM
         The Why
         Purpose                    Know Why
         Insight
         Shared understanding

PAST
         KNOWLEDGE
                                    Know How
         Product
         When to use

         INFORMATION
                                    Know
         Price                      What
         Commodity

         DATA                       Know
         Past performance           Nothing
```

Data: You will notice that data, which sits at the bottom of the pyramid, carries the least value. It is often meaningless in the grand scheme of things, as data can be manipulated and is every changing. This is where performance sits because performance is just data that is already old by the time you get around to talking about it.

Information: Information is only slightly more valuable than data, because information is just data a bit better organized and put into some context. It can inform you in the decision-making process, but you need much more to make great decisions. You can obtain information anywhere from anyone, including the Internet.

Knowledge: Data and information, given meaning and context, can bring some insights, but these insights are also only valuable in the moment. They can change, differ widely from one situation to another, and ultimately may or may not have anything to do with your client's long-term goals or their overriding purpose. It's important to be knowledgeable, but knowledge in and of itself is not enough to separate you from the rest of the advisors out there.

Wisdom: On the Value Pyramid, wisdom sits atop data, information and knowledge. This is wisdom's rightful most valuable perch. Yet many advisors, young and old, continue to focus on the lowest level components of data and information when dealing with their clients. More specifically, they focus on price, performance, and product features without regard to the benefits to the client. This is a limiting endeavor, as these elements bring little value to the advisor-client relationship.

Many people believe wisdom can only be acquired over time. Okay, that may be true to some small extent, but I believe you can learn and acquire wisdom more quickly by focusing on the key elements that make up wisdom and by changing your own perspective. You acquire wisdom by continually focusing on the client's why and consistently bringing insight and purpose to the forefront of the conversation. You are acting wisely when you put the client's best interests before your own. By continually taking the highest altitude view of a situation, you will help yourself put all things in their proper perspective, thereby giving confidence to your client that, while all things are considered, only the highest level goals will be served.

Always strive to elevate what you focus on in client conversations. From this higher level of focus, you can discuss his or her situation in the context of how the client will feel when he or she achieves the goal, fulfills the need, and accomplishes the dream. When you talk with a client at this high altitude level, then price, product, data, and information take on a smaller and more appropriate role in the decision-making process.

By recognizing where your product or service offerings lie in relation to the Value Pyramid, you will learn how to climb the pyramid with your clients. Yes, you will discuss data, respond to information, reveal pricing, and recommend and illustrate products. In isolation, each of these elements enables the client to make a decision potentially without a real purpose. By continually putting these elements in context as you begin to bring your knowledge, expertise and wisdom into play, you ultimately will provide yourself with the platform to pivot to the wisdom conversation: What is your client's high-altitude purpose?

As you develop this ability, you will be able to show up in client meetings as the expert in wanting to understand their needs. You will have the high ground because you will be in a position to support your client's highest-level goals. And you will be providing leadership and "response-ability" by providing your client with perspective and direction. Your relationship will grow deeper, and you will then be positioned as a Wisdom Based Advisor™.

Remember, you are wise! And because you're wise, your job is to always elevate the conversation to the highest-level goals that your client can articulate. And don't forget, strive to be an asker of great questions, an exceptional listener, and a discoverer of your client's dreams.

Before Moving On, Ask Yourself...

1. What can you do to make sure that when talking with clients are you focusing on their highest level goals?

   _____
   _____
   _____
   _____

2. How can you spend more time with clients and prospects talking about their why?

   _____
   _____
   _____
   _____

3. What can you do to become more confident in your own wisdom?

   _____
   _____
   _____
   _____

CHAPTER 6

Managing Your Mindset

"Your beliefs become your thoughts, your thoughts become your words, your words become your actions, your actions become your habits, your habits become your values, your values become your destiny."
—Mahatma Gandhi

As I wrote in an earlier chapter about the six mindsets of success, just a small shift in your thinking can have a huge impact on the trajectory of your future and a big influence on your success. Your mindsets are your truths based on your values and habits, as well as your cumulative life experiences. As with limiting beliefs and the other inner blocks, you can get locked into a mindset—thinking about things in a certain way and believing it's the only way to do things. And why not? This thinking has gotten you to where you are today.

But this thinking can be detrimental to your success because it closes out other possibilities possibilities that can be life-altering. The mindsets that got you where you are today may not be the mindsets that get you to where you want to go in the future. Learning to become more self-aware, more open to possibilities, will help you manage your mindset, which is key to having the outcomes that you want in life. If you can open your mind and change your mindsets, you can change your future!

Your mind is extremely powerful. It would be tempting to say that you would be more successful if you had more education, better sales skills, newer technology, or more staff. The reality is, however, that the space between your ears controls virtually every good or bad outcome in your life. There is a tendency to get busy and get caught up in the day-to-day hustle and forget or overlook the importance of your conscious awareness.

As Earl Nightingale, renowned radio commentator and author of The Strangest Secret said, "We become what we think about most of the time, and that's the strangest secret." For sure, what you think about every day will determine exactly how that day will turn out for you, and you will become what you think about most. Your performance and what you attract in life will be either positive or negative determined by your mindset, beliefs, and behaviors.

But the transformative question is, "How honest can you be with yourself?" To grow, you must be willing to be brutally honest with yourself about where you currently are and where you want to go with your career and your life.

You must be completely clear on this point. Only then can you begin to effectively manage your mindset.

Fixed Mindsets vs. Growth Mindsets

Stanford University psychologist Carol Dweck, in her book *Mindset: The New Psychology of Success*, determined that some people have a "fixed" mindset and believe they cannot change their beliefs or capabilities. Other people have a "growth" mindset and believe they can work toward improving themselves and make significant changes in their lives.

In her research, Dweck and her colleagues studied nearly 400 students and their academic performance through two years of schooling. What they found was that those students with a fixed mindset remained essentially stagnant, while those with a growth mindset were able to raise their grade point averages. I can see this playing out every day with people's mindsets affecting their outcomes in every area of their personal and professional lives.

Dweck goes on to say, "Unfortunately people often LIKE the things that work against their growth. People like to use their strengths to achieve quick, dramatic results even if they aren't developing the new skills they will need later on.

"People also like to believe they are as good as everyone says and not take their weaknesses as seriously as they might. People don't like to hear bad news or get criticism because there is a tremendous risk in leaving what one does well to attempt to master something new.

"If you have a fixed mindset vs. a growth mindset then this seems all that much riskier."

Isn't this so true? Who wants to leave what is familiar and comfortable, and likely somewhat successful, to try new ideas and new methods for doing things that may actually fail in the short run? It sure feels better to keep doing what has worked so far or to adopt short-term fixes to alleviate the disorganization, feelings of being overwhelmed and the constant busyness that agents and advisors so often experience. But to truly grow, some things by necessity will have to change. And changing and learning to manage your mindset is fundamental to your future success—that is, if you want your future to be bigger than what you are currently experiencing.

Inner Blocks and Your Mindset

In Chapter 2, I introduced you to the inner blocks called GAILs (Gremlins, Assumptions, Interpretations, and Limiting Beliefs). I believe that by understanding these inner blocks and how they affect your thinking, attitude, and perceptions, you may hold the key to managing your mindset. Each one of those inner blocks has a profound effect on the form and function of your mindset. Everything you want in life is limited by one of these inner blocks.

The inner dialogue you have with yourself, the constant banter between you and your *Gremlin* serves to limit your vision. The inner talk of your Gremlin is there to keep you nice and safe where you are. But your gut tells you that you can do more, and your heart begs you to take the risk and break out of your comfortable surroundings to go for what you really want. The challenge is that you're fearful. It's natural to feel that way. Learning to manage that self-talk and follow your gut and your heart may feel scary at first, but ultimately you will become more comfortable in your new mindset. I think this is what people are describing when they say, "Go for it!" or "Just do it!" That's easier said than done! But the hope is that by understanding what is behind the fear of making changes, you will be able to get ready to implement your new goals and the changes that will come with your new mindset—the mindset that is aligned with your values and your definition of success.

Consider managing your mindset around the inner block of assumptions. Just because something has happened in the past doesn't need to mean that it will happen again. Your mindset is very much affected by what has happened in the past, and that serves to limit you and your ability to change your way of thinking about the future. Why must it happen that way again? That's the key question.

Can you think of situations where you internally wanted to change or do something differently but felt significant resistance because of your past experiences? That's a strong and scary feeling. I certainly have experienced this in my own life. One such example concerned a new prospect to whom I had been referred. The prospect came into my office, and I met with him and his wife. They were a very nice couple. I thought the meeting went great, but the next day I received a telephone call from the client who had referred the couple to me.

"They liked you well enough," she said, "but they said you talked too much about yourself."

Ouch! That really stung. I was under the assumption that just being myself and sharing that with the prospect was great and was a winning strategy for me. And it usually was, but now I became so self-conscious that I stopped doing it for a while. And I became less effective. I now assumed that if I talked about myself at all, it would be a turn off for prospects. Eventually, I started to overcome this assumption by asking my prospects and clients more questions of a personal nature, which led them to reciprocate and ask me personal questions. I gradually became more comfortable and balanced at revealing my true self, and it eventually became a hallmark of my business. But it was so hard to get past that one episode, which was very bruising to my ego and my confidence. By the way, the prospects in question did become clients, and we developed a great relationship over the years. I never brought up the incident.

Here's something to think about: What could you do if you had no fear? If you are unhappy with the outcomes you are getting but are so bound by your assumptions, ask yourself, "What could I learn to use or do differently that would change the outcome?"

Interpretations, the third inner block, are a key component of your current mindset. In a fixed mindset, interpretations play a large role in keeping you firmly in place where you are. The opinions or judgments you create about an event, a situation, people, or an experience you've had box you into your current thinking and by default limits all other possibilities. The world you experience is a creation of your own perceptions. Simply put, you attract and then see what it is you expect to see. We all see life through our own filters. Therefore it's important, if you are serious about managing and changing your mindset, to examine what a change in your perceptions and a recalibration of your opinions and judgments could do for you in terms of opening up your thinking to new possibilities.

The last of the GAILs, *limiting beliefs*, is almost self-defined. Limiting beliefs are beliefs that you have either bought into or sold yourself on. Think of this in the context of your mindset. This is a powerful block because these beliefs are your truths. To challenge these truths is to challenge your very constitution!

But the beliefs are not necessarily true. They're just what you've come to rely on in your thinking, sometimes to rationalize and justify your behavior or your circumstance. But to grow and change, to accomplish the goals you will set toward the life you want, you will need to challenge your thinking.

You may want to ask yourself the following questions:

- "How true is that belief?"

- "Where did this idea come from?"

- "How can I let go of that belief?"

- "How is this belief affecting me?"

By keeping an open mind in terms of your inner blocks, you will free yourself up to examine your current mindset—fixed or growth—and learn to manage your thinking and reprogram yourself to begin moving in the direction of the success you want. Before you can take a step forward, it's important to look back on the origin of your beliefs, self-talk, and other inner blocks.

Here's an example of how you may apply this thinking to your business. Early in the careers of many agents and advisors, they believe they need to accommodate the unique and singular needs of every prospect and client. They do this because they feel the sheer need to generate any revenues they can just to get their business off the ground. Unfortunately, the end result of operating like this is a lack of efficiencies, which creates profitability problems.

The agent or advisor with a fixed mindset tells himself or herself that the solution to increasing profit is to cut costs or, better yet, grow the business. As it turns out, those issues are usually best addressed not by trying to grow the business itself, which actually can exacerbate the problem, but instead by adopting a growth mindset and changing the business. This requires the agent or advisor to adjust his or her own mindset and perspective away from thinking things have to be done in a certain way– the old way, the way they've always done it in the past. It's like the old joke, "Sell at a loss and make it up in volume!"

The reality is that things don't always need to be done the old way. Fixing the profitability problems in the business by implementing systems, processes, and being more selective in terms of the people with whom you work are the real keys to being more profitable.

And growth can still be a goal. But the growth now will be based on increasing capacity and profit through the adoption of new thinking around efficiency and systems.

Comfort Zone

Comfort zone is a term you have no doubt heard on numerous occasions. "Whoa, I'm way out of my comfort zone here!" That's the common refrain when people find themselves in a situation they aren't used to or prepared for.

Wikipedia defines comfort zone this way: "Comfort zone is a psychological state in which things feel familiar to a person and they are at ease and in control of their environment, experiencing low levels of anxiety and stress. In this zone, a steady level of performance is possible. There is a feeling of having some control."

So can you assume that when you are in your comfort zone you are in a fixed mindset? Fixed mindsets can equal comfort. And the comfort zone sounds like a great place to be, doesn't it? If fact, you can get a lot done when in your comfort zone.

But are you really comfortable, or is there just a familiarity with the way things have always been? Many times, when you are locked into a fixed mindset, you actually may feel uncomfortable because deep down inside you know you aren't where you want to be or need to be, and you aren't living according to your values.

Accordingly, when you begin to adopt a growth mindset, you initially may feel like you are out of your comfort zone, and that would be a natural way to feel. Things may feel unfamiliar to you. You may be challenged by the established order of things and by people resistant to change.

So discomfort can exist within a fixed mindset or a growth mindset.

Although there are benefits to being in the comfort zone and good things can still happen in there, a negative aspect is that you may be missing out on opportunities to experience life more fully and accomplish more. Within the comfort zone, you may be merely surviving, playing it safe, settling for less. Often you're just getting by, procrastinating, and you may experience fear and regret.

If you can see your way to step out of your comfort zone and adopt a growth mindset, it certainly will feel unfamiliar at first. But as you progress, your beliefs and conditioning will change as you adopt new perspectives. What is true for you now may start to shift and things that once caused you fear and discomfort will start to become more familiar and comfortable.

When out of your comfort zone, you will be gaining confidence, choosing happiness, and living without limits. It will be scary at first, but then exciting and fulfilling! By embracing the unknown, you will be going for your dreams and moving toward getting the most out of life.

How will you know if you are moving into a growth mindset? Here are a few questions to ask yourself:

- "Which beliefs no longer serve me?" In reviewing the areas where you are feeling discomfort, fear, frustration, and that feeling of just settling, what are some of the beliefs you are holding that you might may reframe to help you see a way to make some changes to how you see and do these things?

- "Where are my thoughts when I am feeling unsettled?" All people have areas of life where we feel sure-footed, but we also have many areas where deep inside we know we could be doing better and we really want to. But we just feel we can't quite put our fingers on what's missing. Write down some thoughts you have when you are feeling unsettled like this.

- "How would I have to change my thinking to be happier with my results?" Occasionally, when you are settling or just feeling complacent, you just aren't that happy with the results you've been getting because instinctively you know you can do better.

This may require you to revisit how you think about an issue or two. By stopping to identify those results that would make you happier, you may be able to more clearly see what will have to change for you to reach that level of happiness that you desire.

- "What part of my life doesn't fit with who I really am?" Sometimes you may find yourself in a role that just isn't you. You can get into a rut, do things in a mindless and repetitive way, and just feel that if you could be free to be yourself, you would be more productive, happier, and more energized. Take inventory of the places where these feelings show up for you. Define for yourself what things would look like if you could just show up as your true self.

- "What am I unwilling to tolerate any longer?" When fictional television news anchor Howard Beale leaned out of the window, ranting, "I'm mad as hell, and I'm not going to take it anymore!" in the 1976 movie *Network*, he struck a chord with many people. When you are stuck in a situation that doesn't serve you, or blocks you from what you want, it can stifle your creativity and drive. Sometimes you just have to stand up and decide that things will change from now on, regardless of the fallout. If you are in a situation like this, I can tell you that the sooner you take action, the sooner you will feel free to move forward toward what you really want in life.

"Are We There Yet?"

What are the requirements of living with a growth mindset? How will I know when I'm managing my mindset for growth? First, just know that not everything will necessarily change as you adopt new thinking, new perspectives, and different mindsets. For one, your values may stay the same, although they can be fluid. Either way, your values are foundational to your actions and beliefs.

It's your actions that will clue you in as to whether you are making the changes that you really desire and getting the new results you are seeking. Your values are what you will use to measure your progress and your success.

Here are some of the elements that are associated with moving to a growth mindset:

- Dropping old beliefs or changing your perspective around those beliefs.

- Changing and breaking old habits and adopting new ones.

- Adopting new vocabulary. I have a coaching client who was frustrated with his sense of being overwhelmed. I suggested something for him to do about it, and he said, "Yes, I need to do that. I will add that to the list." He didn't even realize that by saying he *needed* to do it that he was further adding to his overwhelmed mentality. By changing the word "need" to "I *want* to do that" or "I *will* do that" his whole outlook changed.

- Adopting or learning new methods for doing things, including delegating and discerning what is required and eliminating what is not required.

- Daily assessment of your progress and checking in on your mindset metrics; asking yourself whether you are comfortable or not, stretched or complacent.

Here are some mindsets that you may expect to experience as you reframe your thoughts and beliefs to that of someone who is successful and who lives with a growth mindset:

- Successful people think, talk, and behave differently than less successful people.

- Successful people don't think about making sales, they think about building relationships.

- Successful people don't talk about their jobs; they work on their business.

- Successful people don't focus just on this week; they are always thinking weeks, months, and years ahead.

- Successful people recognize that what got them to where they are might not get them to where they want to go.

- Successful people stop saying things that are detrimental and start saying things that are beneficial.

- Successful people stop selling features and start selling benefits.

- Successful people stop talking about their clients' performance and start talking about their clients' goals.

- Successful people set growth goals, not comfort goals.

- Successful people stretch; they don't relax.

- When successful people get comfortable, they look to get uncomfortable.

- When living in a growth mindset, you will always remember that how you do anything is how you do everything, and how you see anything is how you see everything.

- When you shift your perspective to a growth mindset, you will shift your life experience and your outcomes.

- The whole idea behind the High Altitude View is to always be aware of your level of thinking and work to shift your perspective to the highest altitude possible to get a clearer view of the big picture.

- Your perspective either creates or sabotages your path to success. And managing your mindset is all about managing your perspective.

So now that you see what is involved in managing you mindset and reprogramming yourself to set new goals and make big changes, the question remains: How do you set these new goals?

In the next chapter, I will share with you some very effective tools to do just that.

Just remember: A new mindset equals new results.

Before Moving On, Ask Yourself...

1. How honest can you be with yourself about where you currently are and where you want to go with your career and your life?

   _____
   _____
   _____
   _____

2. What can you do to align your actions and your mindset with your values and your definition of success?

   _____
   _____
   _____
   _____

3. What could you do with your life if you had no fear?

   _____
   _____
   _____
   _____

CHAPTER 7

Goal Setting and Other Tools

"What you get by achieving your goals is not as important as what you become by achieving your goals."

– Zig Ziglar

As a financial advisor, you are in a unique position. You're a change agent. You can easily speak to the politics of your organization and the legislative challenges within your industry without much effort, and you know you can be a change agent in that arena through donations, engagement, and activism. But more importantly, you're a change agent in the world of your clients, and as such you can have a tremendously positive impact not just on them, but also on your community, on the industry, and on the world. Think about it, if just a few people started thinking about the world as a different place, in a different way, it would have a huge a ripple effect. I believe it's your duty as a leader to use your influence to change not only your life and the lives of those in your immediate family, but your clients' lives, your community, the industry, your company, and anywhere you can.

Change can be hard though, and you will experience resistance from within and without when you initiate change. This happens even though you really want to make changes or you believe strongly that something needs to change. I think this comes from the fact that people get comfortable with the way things are, and it takes a lot of effort to change that momentum.

So what does this have to do with goal setting and achievement? Well, you have to realize that your goals are a glimpse into your future and a big part of the process of change. So becoming clear about how to set great goals, and getting good at it, improves the odds that you will achieve those goals. And after you achieve your goals, you will be that much closer to making the changes that you want in your life—changes that align with your ideal vision of yourself, and success based on your values and your definition of success.

When you are setting goals, it's easy to just blurt out what you want and somehow think you will achieve it, as if by magic: "I want to make a million dollars!" I want to be the best!" "I want to make Top of the Table!"

Most people don't achieve the goals they want to achieve because the goals are ill-defined, are unrealistic, and have no accountability attached to them. Many times the goals are too small, and often times the goals are too large. You set the goals too small so as to increase the odds of reaching the goal, and sometimes you set the goals too large as if the bigger you think, the more legitimate the goal.

The issue here is to find the proper gauge for goal achievement. Good goal achievement requires some serious time spent examining your "why." As I wrote about earlier, after you are clear about your values, who you really are, and what's most important to you, you then can begin to identify what you want to accomplish. But you will never stretch yourself or apply the proper amount of effort to achieving your goals until you are completely clear about why you want to achieve the goal and what it has to do with your success.

I often said to my clients, "You can't get there from here, but you can get here from there." What I meant by that was, knowing where " there" was would enable us to define the steps needed to be taken now in order to put the client on a path toward where they ultimately wanted to be. It helped connect them emotionally to their vision of the future, and that was helpful in motivating them to work hard toward that goal. That can work for you as well.

So let's take a look at a couple of tools that you can use to set, measure, and accomplish your goals in business and in life.

AIM SMART: When attempting to define a goal, either individually or in a group setting, such as within your business or in a committee, the mind almost immediately focuses on the "how." Well," people will ask, "how will that work? How will I do that? How will I afford it?"

These are not really helpful questions at this stage, but this is how most ideas and projects begin. A great phrase I once heard was transformative in how I started looking at and defining my goals: "Transcend the *how*." This perspective simply gives pause to the natural tendency to go to the mechanics of a goal before properly vetting the goal for its worthiness. So try not to get bogged down in that thinking up front and stick with the high-altitude thinking for bit longer.

To give your goal achievement a chance to succeed, I'm going to give you some structure. This structure is called AIM SMART goal setting. AIM SMART is a process for setting goals that contains acceptable (A), ideal (I), and middle (M) action items. It's based on specific (S), measurable (M), achievable (A), reasonable (R), and time-oriented (T) goals. This is not a new concept, by the way. But SMART goals have to do with the quality of the goal that you're setting. It's not good enough just to say, "Oh, I'm going to lose some weight" or "I want to make more money." You have to be specific about your goals.

It is good if you have some initial ideas about the goals you want to achieve, whether they are big life goals, smaller short-term goals, or maybe an intermediate goal, like making the Top of the Table in three years. Regardless, it is important that you are specific about the goal. You can't generalize. The goal has to be measurable.

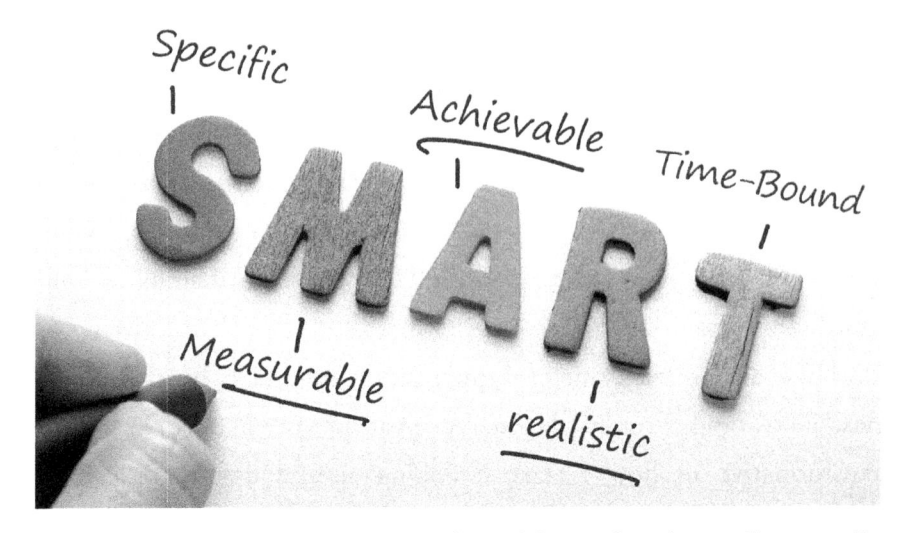

Specific — *Achievable* — *Time-Bound* — *Measurable* — *realistic*

So let's work with the goal of qualifying for the Million Dollar Round Table (MDRT). You know you have a one-year period of time starting in January to accomplish the goal, and you know exactly what the production number is that you're required to reach to accomplish your goal. So there are two SMART criteria right there, and you can check those two boxes—specific and time-oriented.

You also know the goal is achievable. It certainly should be achievable to reach that required level of production as long as you can identify what in your business you need to change, what you need to add, or what you need to do within the allotted time frame in order to achieve it.

Your goal also has to be reasonable. Okay, so is it reasonable to qualify for the MDRT from zero to the end of this year? Depending on which month you begin, that might not be a reasonable goal. But it is certainly reasonable to say, "I've got six months left in the year. I'll get myself into position to make some real changes so that next year I can definitely achieve this goal."

Whatever goal it is for you, as long as it meets these SMART criteria, it's something that you'll have a chance of achieving.

A good goal is time-oriented. You need to put a time limit on it or it will essentially be an open-ended goal, which means you will lack urgency to complete it. You can't just say, "Well, my goal is to someday achieve Court of the Table or Top of the Table."

That's not a realistic goal. That's just a wish or a dream or an intention, but it's not a SMART goal. It needs to be specific, measurable, achievable, reasonable, and time-oriented.

As an additional step toward setting goals, I include the AIM process. Again, AIM stands for acceptable, ideal, and middle action items. The AIM process breaks down your SMART goals into these action items. To illustrate how this would work, consider the example of going to the gym. Let's say your goal is to get to the gym to meet your SMART goal of losing ten pounds in the next month. You already know that your specific goal is to lose ten pounds, so to start going to the gym as a means to achieve that weight loss is an acceptable goal.

What's the acceptable absolute minimum action that you can take? Well, let's say you're not going to the gym at all now, so if you went one day, that's the minimum you could do and that would be progress. The ideal would be for you to go five or six days a week to the gym. That would be ideal, but maybe that's not reasonable given the way things are set up in your life right now.

So, what's the middle action that you could take? The middle is that you could commit to going three days a week. At its core it's a matter of getting real about your goals. And the AIM exercise is the action part, or implementation part, of your SMART goal.

After you qualify your goal according to SMART, and you know that you have a legitimate goal that meets all the SMART criteria, then you can go on to the next step and do the AIM part of the process, where you actually put things into action. This tool will work on any goal. By using the AIM SMART process, you will discover that your dreams start to become realities and you will make progress toward what you really want in your business and in life.

I used the AIM SMART method when I was training for running a marathon. It went something like this. My specific goal was to run the 26.2 mile Marine Corp Marathon, one of the biggest, most challenging, and most popular races in the United States. Actually, people entered from all over the world. The race was in October of that year, and I set the goal in March.

I had to decide whether it was truly achievable for me given my age and physical condition. I decided that it was doable, as I was in decent shape and had run long races before, including a half marathon.

Was it realistic? Yes. I had plenty of time to get in shape and train for the race.

How was it measurable? Well, I discovered that there were several books available that actually set out training schedules for each day, week, and month, and the schedules were adaptable to the amount of time available to train before the race. So I was able to measure my progress by documenting and logging my training runs and other related training into the book.

Finally, it was indeed time bound, as the race was to be run in October, rain or shine! I did run a couple of 26-mile training runs in preparation for the race. And I did step up to the starting line for the marathon on one of the most beautiful and ideal days for running a race.

Unfortunately, at about mile nine, my knee collapsed, and I was hauled off the race course in an ambulance due to a torn meniscus, a membrane, in my knee. After surgery on the knee I never ran again, but I always will have those two training runs to show for my efforts, knowing in my heart that I could've done it were it not for the injury.

And I proved to myself that I could set and achieve big goals in my life regardless of the outcome. After all, my goal was to run the race, not to win, and not necessarily to finish. There are lots of great takeaways from that experience!

The GROW model: There is another method available to you for goal setting and problem solving. It's called the GROW model. This model was developed in the late 1980s in the United Kingdom, and it may also prove to be useful to you in some of your personal and business goal setting.

There are several different versions of the GROW model. The image below presents one view of the stages, but there are some others out there. The "O" in this version could have two meanings—either options, obstacles, or both.

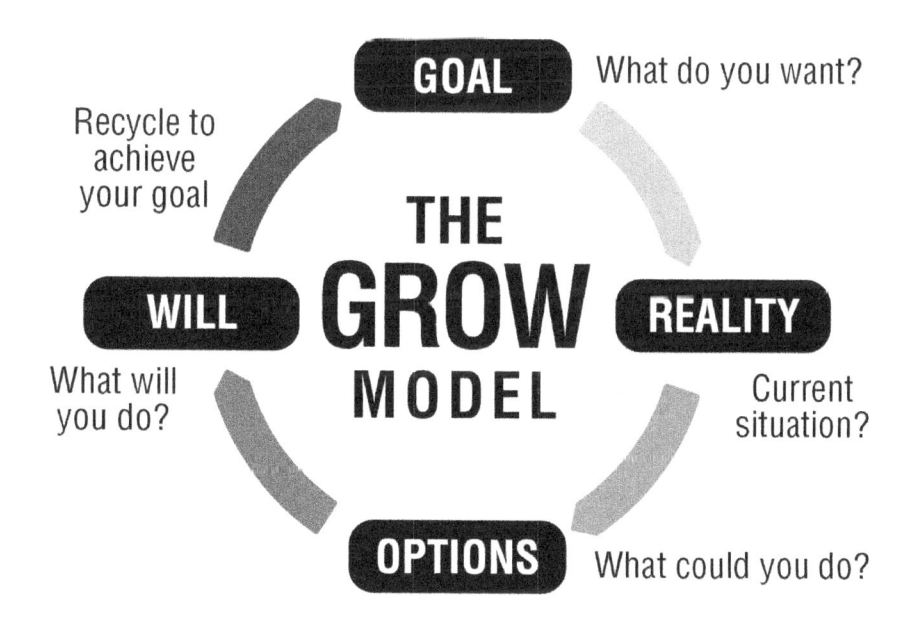

THE GROW MODEL

- **GOAL** — What do you want?
- **REALITY** — Current situation?
- **OPTIONS** — What could you do?
- **WILL** — What will you do?
- Recycle to achieve your goal

As with many simple principles, anyone who decides to use the GROW model for goal setting and achievement can apply their own skill and knowledge at each stage of the process. But the basic process works as illustrated in the graphic above.

Let's consider a very simple example of using the GROW model to achieve a goal. This example deals with losing weight. If you want to bring your weight down 20 pounds in three months and keep it down, that is your goal (G). The more aligned your goal is with your personal values, the more meaningful the goal will be to you and the more likely you will be to commit to and achieve the goal.

The next step in the GROW approach would then be to assess and document the reality (R) of the situation by stating what your weight is now. It would be helpful to ask yourself awareness questions to deepen your understanding of what is happening when you try to lose weight, because this helps you identify any obstacles (O) to achieving the goal. Ask yourself some "reality check" questions like these:

- "When have I been able to lose weight in the past, and what made the difference?"

- "What are the differences between the times I was able to keep weight off and the times when I just put it back on again?"

- "What would I have to change to be sure I could lose the weight and keep it off this time?"

If you can honestly answer these questions, you might discover some new information concerning what works and what doesn't work for you in terms of weight loss, and that knowledge can create some potential for change. It then becomes possible to create some strategies or options (O) that could possibly help you maneuver around the obstacles (O). These options could include looking at which diets or exercise regimes work best for you, or finding some kind of support, such as a trainer, nutritionist, or coach.

After you discover the strategies that are likely to work for you, then you can establish a way forward (W), which involves taking action steps. In other words, what are you willing (W) to do? This is where you commit to what you will do in the short term to put the strategies into place. For instance, one action might be asking a friend or relative for support, and another might be to start buying and eating different foods.

I use the GROW model in my coaching practice because it neatly highlights the nature of a problem for coaching purposes. In order for a problem to exist in coaching terms, there have to be two elements present. First, there has to be something that my client is trying to achieve—that is, his or her goal (G). Then there has to be something stopping the client from achieving that goal—the obstacle (O) or obstacles (O). The GROW model automatically breaks a problem down into these two component parts.

You can apply these same principles to whatever goal or problem you might have. You can use the GROW model on technical problems, issues regarding processes, strategic questions, interpersonal issues, and much more.

One of the techniques that I use is to keep records to track my progress toward my goals and to turn that progress into motivation. For instance, in sales I would make a list of the goals I wanted to accomplish, the obvious obstacles to achieving those goals, and the results of the efforts that I made. When I had identified a prospect, the steps needed to make the sale, and the results of the sale, I would keep a running tally of how much I had earned toward my annual goals and my MDRT qualification. Sure, sometimes I didn't make the sale, but just by adding up and measuring what I did accomplish and overcome, I found it immensely gratifying and motivating.

I do the same thing in other aspects of my life, such as when I decide to lose weight or to become more fit. I record my goal, and I measure my progress. Then I review that progress to keep myself motivated.

There certainly are other methods for goal achievement, but regardless of what method you use, your goals need to be documented; hurdles to accomplishing the goals acknowledged; support, money, or systems needed to accomplish the goal identified; and progress tracked so that it can be celebrated.

Going back to the basics, let's think about why you want and need to set goals. The high altitude view is that in some areas of your life, you are not happy or satisfied with the way things currently are. Therefore, you feel the need to change the way you are thinking or do things differently so that you can achieve different outcomes—the outcomes you desire. You can identify those outcomes by defining your values, setting boundaries to block those activities and behaviors that don't align with your values, and defining your mission—what you want and why you want it.

By setting goals and using the methods I have shared here, you will ensure that your goals are realistic and aligned with your vision. Regardless of how you do it or which system you use, my intention in this chapter is to teach you to be able to quantify your goals, qualify them, and then create positive action steps around them so that you actually can achieve your goals.

If you will follow this process, you will experience the changes you want and achieve the outcomes you envision. But as the adage goes, "Be careful what you ask for; you just might get it."

I encourage you to define your *who*, decide on your *what* – that is, your goal—and know *why* you want to accomplish that goal.

Before Moving On, Ask Yourself...

1. What will it look like when you accomplish your biggest life goals?

___

2. What do you need that you don't currently have to reach your goals?

___

3. Imagine that it is one year from today, and you've achieved your biggest goals. Write down what that will feel like.

___

CHAPTER 8

With Change Comes Challenges

"The secret to change is to focus all of your energy, not on fighting the old, but on building the new."

– Socrates

Now that you know how to manage your mindset and how to actually set and achieve goals, you are ready to make the big changes in your life and your business that you've been thinking of, worrying about, and dreaming of for so long. And you can feel confident that you have the drive and the ability to make these changes for yourself. Really, you don't need anyone's permission to effect changes to your business or life. You will just want to be aware that, as you change, you may experience some challenges that you did not anticipate.

While many people will be cheering you on, not everyone in your circle of friends and associates is going to be as excited about all the changes that you are making in your life as you make them. In fact, it's one of those dirty little secrets out there—many people actually will want you to stay right where you are in life, because it serves their purpose and fits neatly into their view of the world. Your reaching your full potential would upset the applecart and might, God forbid, impact them and how they operate and interact with you.

Don't get me wrong, people won't try to stop you necessarily, but they may feel free to point out to you all the reasons why your new goals and dreams won't work or actually pan out. Don't hold it against them; it's just human nature.

I wrote about the comfort zone in Chapter 6, where I addressed managing your mindset, and that comfort zone can come into play in this kind of situation. You see, when everyone and everything stays the same, usually those people you know can feel comfortable in that they know where they stand with you and what is required of them. But when you start to change things around, those people may feel insecure, jealous, frightened, and sometimes angry. That's because you are changing the status quo.

I don't point this out to discourage you, but rather to raise your self-awareness around this phenomenon. In my own experience, when I made substantial changes in the way I did business or conducted my life, I was met with resistance almost every time. But I didn't let it stop me. I knew in my heart that the changes that I wanted to make were coming from a strong desire, indeed a burning need, to do things differently so that I could be more aligned with my own values and my own natural way of seeing the world and how I fit into it.

When I started out in sales, I was a very different person than I am today. I was not confident, and I was somewhat insecure. This caused me to just go along with what I was taught, and told to do. And frankly, that served me pretty well for a while. But as I gained confidence, my insecurities went away and I began to think about doing things differently in the sense that I felt that maybe my way would be better—for me.

The Only Constant

Now would be a good time to consider change in the broader sense. There is change that you make, and there is change that happens, which you did not initiate or even desire. Heraclitus, a Greek philosopher, was quoted as saying, "Change is the only constant in life." That means that change *will* happen. The only question is about whether you initiated the change or the change was initiated by an outside influence. Either way, how you respond to change and the perspective that you adopt around the change will determine how successful you will be as you navigate the changes. Socrates said, "The secret to change is to focus all of your energy, not on fighting the old, but on building the new."

I have always believed that adaptability is the most important life skill. Your ability to adapt to change determines how successful your outcomes will be. This is true whether you are initiating the change or the change comes from elsewhere.

I experienced remarkable changes during my financial services career of nearly 40 years. When I started out, there were no computers! I used to drive around in the country outside the small southern town where I was living and collect insurance premiums door to door. Can you imagine? I drove miles and miles while listening to an 8-track tape player in my car. I only had one tape and that was *Led Zeppelin IV*. I can still play a mean air guitar to "Stairway to Heaven," having listened to it hundreds of times while covering my territory.

My job was to collect the premiums, like a paper route, and then try to sell more life insurance while I was at the house. Then, I was expected to go to the next house and cold call to try to create a new customer. It was a brutal way to earn a living. I was met at the door by some interesting people, who mostly slammed the door in my face. Occasionally, I was invited in for a piece of pie or coffee, and sometimes

I made a new sale. I like to joke that I became quite keen at discerning the sound of the click of a deadbolt lock and the click of a 12-gauge shotgun!

My next move was to work for an "upscale" life insurance company in Washington, DC—a big city and a big change. For a while it was pretty much the same routine except that my clients had more money and bigger needs. And I didn't need to drive around so much. But I still had to cold call and try to develop new sales on my own. And still there were no computers.

The first big change I experienced was at this insurance company. One day, out of the blue, we were informed that we were getting computers and that we would be getting trained on how to create illustrations to use in presenting product proposals. That caught a lot of the older agents off guard, to say the least, and some left the company. Many of my younger peers and I took it in stride and actually were curious and interested in this new technology. Little did I know at that time that 30-plus years later I would use technology to operate my business virtually, with no physical office or paper files, and serve my clients in more than 20 different states from my home on the water in Maryland!

Shortly after the installation of computers in our office, we were informed that all the agents would be expected to study for and attain a Series 7 securities license. We couldn't believe it. Weren't we just an insurance company selling insurance? Nope, not anymore.

This is where I responded with fear. I never fancied myself to be a great test taker, and I immediately adopted a Level 1 perspective of being a victim and became fearful and indifferent. This was a poor response, because acquiring the Series 7 license would turn out to be one of the best things that ever happened to me—eventually.

Because I had such a negative response to the idea, I didn't properly prepare for the test and I failed it. In fact, I failed it three times before I finally passed it. I took me three times not because I wasn't smart, but because I had such a fear-based response that it affected my perspective on the whole opportunity.

Many of the older agents in the company either retired or left the company as their response. I wasn't in a position to do that and, in hindsight, had I been able to shift my perspective fairly quickly to Level 5, where opportunity is the dominant thought, I would have avoided so much fear, pain, and embarrassment. Unfortunately for me, at that time, I wasn't aware of the Seven Levels of Perspective and how I could shift my perspective to a High Altitude View. Partly because of my immaturity and partly because of my insecurities, I didn't handle that first big change particularly well.

Jack Canfield, author of the series of *Chicken Soup for the Soul* books, offers these tips to embrace change:

- Always believe it's possible to create positive outcomes.

- See yourself as already being the kind of person who can successfully adapt to any kind of change.

- Acknowledge your fears, but take action anyway.

Fast-forward a few years to the late 1980s. With the full integration of technology into the financial services business came the advent of what we now know as financial planning. It was a new discipline that resembled needs-based insurance planning but was much more comprehensive to include investment advice.

This was something that made so much sense to me and something that I was well-suited for. By this time, I was able to adapt more easily to the change, and I embraced it successfully—so much so that I decided to leave the insurance company to join a financial planning firm and started charging fees for advice, in addition to selling insurance and other financial products.

That position lasted 12 years, and I learned a lot from my partner. During the last couple of years of that job, I started participating in the Strategic Coach program. It opened my eyes to many new perspectives. Almost immediately, I knew that I no longer belonged in that partnership and decided, for the first time in my life, to start my own business.

It was ugly. Remember how I mentioned that some people wouldn't respond well to your changes and growth? Well, my former partner took it personally and got very angry and defensive. He actually did, initially, try to impede my move. He was threatened by it and fearful of what it may cost him. It took a toll on our relationship.

But my values were driving my decision to move on. It was my need to be more aligned with my values and adopt a way of doing business that was completely congruent with the way I thought it ought to be done, for me, that caused me to stick to my guns and move on. Fortunately, over the years, my former partner and I got through the episode and are now able to maintain a good relationship.

That was a very challenging time in my career, but it validated my belief in myself and gave me yet another opportunity to see change in a different light. By this time, I had "survived" some significant changes in my career and actually had seen how those changes had given me a new outlook on life. Those experiences gave me confidence to effect changes more readily with less resistance and hesitation than in the past. And this is what will happen to you as you embrace change and manage your mindset around the change and other's reactions to your new vision.

Clearly, there were plenty of other changes that occurred during my career, such as hiring and firing employees, changing broker dealers, moving offices, signing leases, getting bigger clients, losing big clients, growing my book of business, and then intentionally trimming my book for efficiency. And that's not to mention adopting technology to transform my business. I actually moved from struggling to survive in the business to making more money than I ever imagined and creating my own successful investment advisory and financial planning firm.

In my personal life, we managed changes in my wife's career, raised three children, bought cars and homes, moved several times, lost loved ones, celebrated the good times, and mourned those lost. Each life event brought more opportunity for perspective. After you embrace change and learn to manage your response to it, you actually will start to look for opportunities to experience change, you'll get better at navigating it, and you will see the power in developing and adopting a growth mindset.

The Cycle of Change*

Change is such an interesting and curious word that can generate a diverse reaction in people. Many people absolutely love change and thrive on what it can bring to their lives. Other people strive to simply cope with and survive change. Still others will do whatever possible to avoid change.

A lot of the resistance to change comes from perspective. Although you can understand at an intellectual level that all change is natural and an inevitable part of life, that curiosity and understanding can disappear pretty quickly when change shows up at your door. The main thing to remember is that there is a process and a four-phase cycle to change, and understanding this can help to alter your perspective about it and give you the tools to manage it.

In the first phase of change, you may experience an emotional setback in the sense that you realize that life will be different from now on. It's a time when you realize that something is ending—the "old way"—and something new is beginning. You may start to take stock of the situation, and you might experience a sense of fear of the unknown. This is a time for you to evaluate your options, review your values, and decide what's most important before you decide which direction to go and how to respond. This phase involves letting go of what was, facing your fear of the unknown, understanding your options, embracing the possibilities, and making plans to adapt.

The second phase of change is an action phase. This is a period where you are now starting to deal with the fact that change is happening in the sense that you will start to implement the plans that you contemplated in phase one. Although you may have embraced the change to some extent, you are still likely to have a cautious, "one step at a time" mentality. Your self-talk might sound something like, "Sure, I'll try it, but I don't want to go all in yet."

When you are in this stage, you may start to feel more confident about the outcomes of the change and also might start to actually get a little bit excited. Here, you are starting to reestablish expectations, while looking for clarity, process, and support.

The third phase of change is a mainly positive time in the cycle, when you are fully implementing your new plan. This can be a time of successes, but you could also experience setbacks, disappointments, and new challenges. You could have feelings of self-doubt and could still have feelings of fear of failure and inadequacy. The main thing to remember here is to refocus on your values and check your perspective. You get to choose how you respond and how you elevate your perspective. You control your attitude, and you will want to remember one of the six mindsets for success that I shared with you—failure is the secret sauce of success!

The fourth phase of success is the last stage of the cycle. All things come to an end in this world. Sometimes it ends with a failure and sometimes it ends with a success. Either way, people aren't usually ready for the cycle to end.

Whether it's the end of a job, a relationship, or any aspect of a goal or a project, when you get to this phase of the cycle of change you can feel accomplished, but you will often be unhappy and unsure of what is coming next. To make sense of this cycle, think of it in terms of expectations. Say things were going along just fine, and then you were presented with, or decided to make, a change. You are unsure of how it will work out. Maybe you're fearful or maybe you are excited, but either way, you try to adjust and see the possibilities. Then you accept the change and start to make a plan and implement that plan.

You either have success or a setback or some of both. If the plan succeeds, you are happy, but you also may realize that the change didn't fix or solve all of your problems. Or maybe it did. Either way, you are now back at the beginning of the cycle where the next change is waiting for you. Assess, adjust, take action, and accept the outcome. Repeat.

Now that you know that change has a cycle associated with it, you will be better equipped to manage your feelings and fears as well as the reactions and rejections of others that may be involved in or affected by the change. I hope this will help you manage your mindset and adjust your perspective.

As I have said, change can be very exciting, but it also can be incredibly stressful and bring real challenges and conflicts. Remember that what creates blocks for one person may be a source of inspiration for another.

Here are some obstacles and influencers to be aware of that will help you manage change and the challenges it can bring:

- *Belief and Value Systems*: Your core beliefs and values will cause you to view change as either and opportunity, something to survive, or something to resist. When you are feeling out of sorts, take stock of your values and beliefs to see where you can make an adjustment in line with your values to help you with the change.

- *Relationships at work and home*: How the people in your life—bosses, peers, associates, clients or family—react to your change can have a positive or negative effect on how you respond. Just be aware of this and let your values and beliefs drive your decisions.

- *Environment*: Your physical environment can affect your outlook. To keep your energy positive, take care to maintain appropriate privacy, personal space, and professional appearances, all of which can influence your thinking positively.

- *Health and wellness*: Your physical, emotional, and spiritual states can impact your thinking and either can enhance or detract from your attitude and willingness to embrace change. Commit to taking care of yourself so that you can be the best you that you can be.

- *New interests and new priorities*: Let your values drive your decisions and your direction as much as you can. Remember the importance of "who, what, and why." Things change but knowing *who* you really are, *what* you really want, and *why* you really want it will serve as a benchmark for all your decisions and responses around changes that you initiate or face.

In the end, you have options as to how you deal with change and any conflict that may come from it. Let's reference the seven levels of attitudinal perspectives as your review the options. You can choose any of the following:

- *Remain a victim to it*: You are choosing a Level One response, living as though life and the change or conflict in particular is happening *to* you. You are choosing to detach and suffer, likely hurting no one but yourself and possibly missing out on an opportunity for growth.

- *Avoid the change or conflict*: Refusing to engage is still a Level One response and mindset. Sometimes it's no fun to address something that can be upsetting or painful, but eventually, usually, the change or conflict will have to be dealt with. In my experience, the sooner you deal with it, the less painful it will be.

- *Change the situation*: This is an action-oriented position. Level Two and Level Three perspectives come into play here. Now you are ready to deal with the situation at hand. You are no longer willing to accept the status quo and you are going to address the situation and get involved to create a favorable outcome for yourself and perhaps others. It might get ugly or messy, but you are resolved to change it so things work out for you at least, and ideally, for all involved.

- *Change your perspective of the experience*: Here, you would be adopting the mindsets of levels Three, Four, and Five. You are now looking at the change or conflict in terms of how you may be able to compromise, help others involved (even if at your own expense), and look for opportunities for everyone to benefit from the situation. You realize that you have the ability to respond, learn from the experience, and take a High Altitude View of the situation to make the best of it for everyone involved.

- *Accept it*: This is a Level Six and even Level Seven response. You understand that change is part of life and that you are adaptable. It doesn't impact you negatively because you realize that, in the game of life, this will happen over and over again, and that it may even be the best thing that ever happened to you. And in the end, it doesn't even matter because whatever it is will change yet again sometime in the future. You take the positives from it and you keep moving, not letting the situation slow you down from reaching your high-level, values-driven goals.

Whether setting new goals and initiating changes or facing change you did not seek, it's beneficial for you to take stock of what you control and what you don't. One thing is for certain; you always have control of your response, your attitude, and your perspective. As motivational speaker Zig Ziglar said, "It's your attitude, not your aptitude that determines your altitude!"

Even though change can be hard at times, and challenging, don't let that stop you, because change is where your growth comes from. If things get tough, step back and take a High Altitude View of the situation, inventory your values, and remember your why.

Before Moving On, Ask Yourself…

1. If you were to make big changes in your business and life, what do you think will happen?

___

2. If you had all the time, energy, and money to achieve your goals, what would you do?

___

3. What's stopping you from being all that you believe you can be?

___

* *The Cycle of Change was created by Bruce D. Schneider of iPEC® and is used with permission.*

CHAPTER 9

Your New Mindset and Leadership

"The challenge of leadership is to create change and facilitate growth."
— John C. Maxwell

I have written a lot in this book about mindsets, change, and perspective. That's because these are the elements of personal growth, success, and happiness. So why a chapter on leadership? Because now that you have been exposed to a way of defining success for yourself, addressing your inner blocks, changing your perspective, and managing your mindset, you will become one very attractive person.

I'm not talking about becoming attractive in the physical sense. I am talking about becoming attractive in the energetic sense. People naturally will be drawn to you now that you are someone who is in control of your emotions and your attitudes and *who* knows who you are, *what* you want, and *why* you want it. You are now someone who understands the power of managing your mindset and who now knows how to set and achieve big goals.

And you have learned what it means to be "response-able." As such, you will become influential to the people in your office and your community, and to your associates and clients as well. This is because people are looking to be led by those who have vision. They want a confident person to lead the way, because as you may have experienced, making the big internal and mental changes that you are making is not easy to do. Not everyone wants to be a leader, but almost everyone, I believe, wants to follow one. We are starving for leadership in this world, and guess what? That leader is you!

So you've never thought of yourself as leader? That's okay, because most people don't think of themselves that way, even if other people see them that way. I think it's fair to say at this point that it's a myth that good leaders are born, not made. Good leaders are self-aware and brutally honest with themselves. They recognize the Seven Attitudinal Perspectives, and know how to shift their perspective almost at will. They understand the GAILs and how to avoid being limited by those inner blocks. They instinctively take the High Altitude View in critical situations. And they know how to manage their mindsets. So do you.

What is Leadership?

The American scholar Warren Bennis, organizational consultant and author who is widely regarded as a pioneer of the contemporary field of leadership studies, said, "Leadership is the capacity to translate vision into reality."

And isn't that what we have been talking about throughout this entire book, trying to make the vision you have of your future and the futures of those you care about become reality? Knowing what you know now gives you that ability and that capacity, so by definition you are a leader.

Another simple definition is that leadership is the art of motivating a group of people to act toward achieving a common goal. This definition points out the essential elements of being able to inspire others and being willing and prepared to do so. Effective leadership is based on ideas—and vision—but it can't happen unless those ideas and vision can be communicated to the people within their sphere of influence in a way that will engage them enough to motivate them to act in the way you want them to act.

The bottom line is that a leader is the inspiration and initiator of the action. A leader is a person who possesses the combination of personality and skills that make others want to follow his or her direction.

For many of us, when we hear the term leadership, we usually think of CEOs, managers, elected officials, or other influential people. But becoming a leader doesn't require a specific job title. In theory, we're all leaders, every day, in every area of our lives. John Maxwell, a leading thinker in the area of leadership says, "Leadership is not about titles, positions or flowcharts. It is about one life influencing another."

This means that no matter who you are or what you do, you have the opportunity to lead when interacting with another person. The question really isn't, "Are you a leader?" The question really is, "How skillfully can you lead in your everyday life?"

Everyday leaders are parents, partners, teachers, therapists, caregivers, entrepreneurs, human resources managers, consultants, general managers, branch managers, advisors…the list goes on and on. *

Think of roles where you might attach the word "leader" to get a better understanding of the meaning:

- Leader of the choir at church.
- Team leader for cookie sales for the Girl Scouts.
- Senate Majority Leader.
- Leader of the free world.
- Leader in the race.
- Leader and organizer of a book club.
- Leader of a running, exercise, or yoga group.

- Group leader in a Bible study.
- Leader and organizer of a neighborhood dinner club.
- Leader of a volunteer group or local charity.
- Leader (or co-leader) of your family.
- Leader of your child's school's PTA or PTO.

Why it's Important to See Yourself as a Leader

Everyone is a leader, at least in certain settings, so it makes sense to view yourself as such. Given the tremendous self-awareness that you now possess and the influence that you have with the people in your life, people will see you as a leader. You have the opportunity to use your new skill sets to help other people make progress in their lives, just as you are trying to do both personally and professionally.

To clarify, there are many applications of leadership within the corporate world, as well as in the world of non-corporate activities. There are many books, articles, and white papers devoted to this highly nuanced subject matter. My intention here is not to teach you all about leadership of all kinds and subsets. My goal is to help you realize that you are a leader and as such you have an obligation to get involved and to get out in front for the sake of your family, clients, staff, and industry. I believe everyone needs to take his or her turn carrying the torch. What you have, in terms of material things, financial security, and opportunity likely came about by your hard work, but much of the groundwork was probably laid by someone before you. Or at least you likely received assistance in some way from people in your life who realized their leadership responsibilities.

To view oneself as a leader means that you will be embracing the role and the responsibilities that come with leadership.

Here are some mindsets and attitudes of a responsible leader:

- Leaders take their current responsibilities seriously.
- Leaders don't commit to doing more than they can handle.
- Leaders acknowledge their mistakes, and they don't make excuses.
- Leaders follow through and finish what they start.
- Leaders take time to consider how they can help others.
- Leaders always maintain an optimistic outlook.
- Leaders consider the consequences when they make tough decisions.
- Leaders are not afraid to make a mistake.

Many of these mindsets and attitudes seem almost obvious, but I am willing to bet that you have worked with or for "leaders" who were missing one or more of these mindsets and attitudes, and I'm sure you can see how that could be an issue in many situations. These mindsets and perspectives are, to my mind, fundamental. Yet they don't go far enough to set the great leaders apart from the good leaders.

Great leaders take an even higher altitude view and hold these beliefs:

- Great leaders feel obliged to earn their position.
- Great leaders strive to leave their organization in better shape than they found it.
- Great leaders always seek to set a positive example for others.
- Great leaders hold themselves to a high level of ethics and integrity.

- Great leaders learn from their mistakes.
- Great leaders cope well with problems.
- Great leaders are not afraid to ask tough questions.
- Great leaders consider all involved when making decisions.

The Advisor as a Leader

Where will you be seen as a leader? There are many arenas where you will be seen as a leader or where you can decide that your leadership can be helpful and beneficial.

Leadership in your family

First, let's start within your own family. Regardless of your position within the family—father, mother, sister or brother—you can begin by behaving like a leader, using the mindsets I have listed above. As a spouse, your partner looks to you for selflessness and support, objectivity but gentle truth. Far be it from me to describe a perfect marriage, but it was once told to me that marriage was a process of mutual subordination. I take that to mean that neither is more important that the other. And yet the mentality is the opposite; the other's needs are more important in your mind.

Each of you will have different strengths and weaknesses, but in the grand scheme, as a leader, you will have the opportunity almost constantly to rise above the petty, take the High Altitude View, and do and say what is right for all the right reasons. That's what a leader does.

By the way, this leadership behavior sets a wonderful example for your children, if you have them. If you happen to be an adult child dealing with your siblings or perhaps aging parents, leadership opportunities are abundant. When in doubt about how to bring your positive influence to a family dynamic, simply review the leadership traits and mindsets above as a reference. The short list includes objectivity, respect, deference, and love.

Leadership in your business

It should go without saying that, as the head of your business or the owner of the company, you are by default the leader. At least that is your role, if not yet your mentality. Having said that, I know that in real life those in this position don't always embrace that mantle.

I had this discussion recently with a coaching client. He was frustrated at some of the actions of his staff and had recently lost a sales associate. I inquired about his interactions with these folks and how he saw himself in terms of his role as the leader of the organization. His response was typical. "I set up regular times to meet with my staff," he said. "But many times, the meetings get pushed back and postponed because a sales opportunity comes up, and sales are more important."

Hmmm, I thought. Really now. If this happens to sound familiar, don't be alarmed. Many people in the "sales" world really love to sell. It's thrilling at times and just the interaction with clients and prospects almost always energized me for days. But as a business owner or leader of an organization, selling is just one aspect of your job. You simply must pay attention to your role as a leader to get the best out of your employees, to empower them and inspire them. This is a function every bit as important as selling, just not always as exciting.

Many advisors prefer to sell and see clients, and managing and leading their staff are just a pain! "Just let me do my job and sell. You guys know what to do; now just do it!"

When I hear someone say this, I remind him or her that managing is your job, and leading is your job. You are a business owner, and as such, you must pay attention to these functions. Now, if the role you play in your organization doesn't involve management or supervision, that's another issue. But I am assuming here that you have people you need to support you in your selling endeavors, and when that is the case, it's time for a shift in your thinking.

So how can you reframe the issue to get the same or similar levels of reward and excitement from leading that you get from selling? Think about all the things you love about selling and the feelings around those things. What do you love about selling? What part of leading and managing do you love? What part of each function do you dislike?

I'm willing to wager that there are some common themes in those answers. The thing is, you will have to figure out sooner or later a way to cover all three functions of selling, managing, and leading. Hire a manager to take care of the staff? Okay. Now you just need to sell and lead. Hire someone to sell, and you manage? Okay, but you still need to be a leader. Hire someone to manage and sell? Yep.... still a leader. But even if you did just some of these things to some degree, your business would probably skyrocket.

Remember what I wrote about in Chapter 4, The Six Mindsets of Success. Remember the part about giving up control? Reread that part in the context of your staffing or sales associate retention issues, and I think you will see some of what is going on there. The bottom line is that the issues will not go away because you are avoiding them. Place a similar weight of importance on selling as you do on your interaction with your employees, and you will see improvements. Because when you own the leadership mentality and you engage and communicate with the people within your span of influence, you are almost guaranteed to see progress.

Remember, people want to be led, and they want to be inspired.

You are a leader to your clients

Your clients have come to you for advice and for help in making financial decisions of many kinds. They hired you for many possible reasons—because you came recommended, or they thought you were the best, or because they trusted you, or because your fees were most fair, or because you were close to where they lived and had free parking. The fact of the matter is that you will keep them only as long as all those things are still true, unless you become their leader.

When they see you as their leader, they will follow you and give you the benefit of the doubt when things eventually come up that cause them to consider moving. And that will happen. You are successful in their eyes, and they want what you have. They want the life you are creating for yourself and you are helping them to get that.

I shared my life with my clients as much as I could. I invited clients to my home, sometimes for overnight stays, and sometimes to the weddings of our daughters. In turn, I was invited to their homes and their children's weddings. I tried to take care of my clients by helping them make good buying decisions around things like cars or houses. They would ask me things like, "Where did you buy your car?" or "Who does your mortgage?" Many times a client would buy the same car as me! And they took comfort in knowing that if the mortgage person I was using was good enough for me, then it was good enough for them.

Some clients bought the same watch I wore, and some clients bought similar glasses. Why? Because I was transparent, relatable, and accessible to them. They saw me walking my talk. I was leading a life they saw as a good life, and they wanted to follow and have that life too.

I had credibility with them because I was following my own advice. And when hard times would come, they gave me the benefit of the doubt and stuck with me.

That creates a strong bond between you and your clients. By realizing your role in their lives as a leader, you will rise above any competition you may perceive yourself to have. You will become a better advisor because you will employ all the mindsets and attitudes of a leader and these characteristics and qualities will set you apart from other advisors. Take the risk, if you perceive it as such, to mentally take the lead and show your people the way—your way—to get them where they want to go. This is the thinking of a wisdom-based advisor, an advisor who brings high altitude thinking to the table.

You are a leader in your industry and your community

I know from experience that there are myriad opportunities to get involved in your community and in the financial services industry. Your local National Association of Insurance and Financial Advisors (NAIFA) chapters in the United States have many jobs that need volunteers, and I am sure this is true in similar organizations in other countries. These volunteer positions also many times involve doing something that benefits the local community, and that's a real win-win.

Volunteering in general brings about many benefits, but one of the best is the chance to practice your leadership skills and mindset. The Million Dollar Round Table (MDRT) annual meeting and related meetings throughout the world bring forth so many volunteering opportunities that it is extremely easy to get involved. And with those opportunities comes more chances to develop your leadership skills.

As I wrote earlier, I believe that we all benefit from those who came before us and did the heavy lifting in our communities and our industry. Raise your hand to volunteer and roll up those sleeves to put in your time. I promise you will be rewarded through the good you do, the people you meet, and the friends you will make. And you will rise to leadership before you know it.

Elements of a great leader

I created The Wheel of Great Leadership below as a way to graphically illustrate the elements of what I consider to be great leadership. I have covered a lot of territory relating to leadership in this chapter, but it is a subject so broad and so deep that entire books have been written and curricula developed around the issue. My intent with the graph is to give you a quick reference for use in your own life.

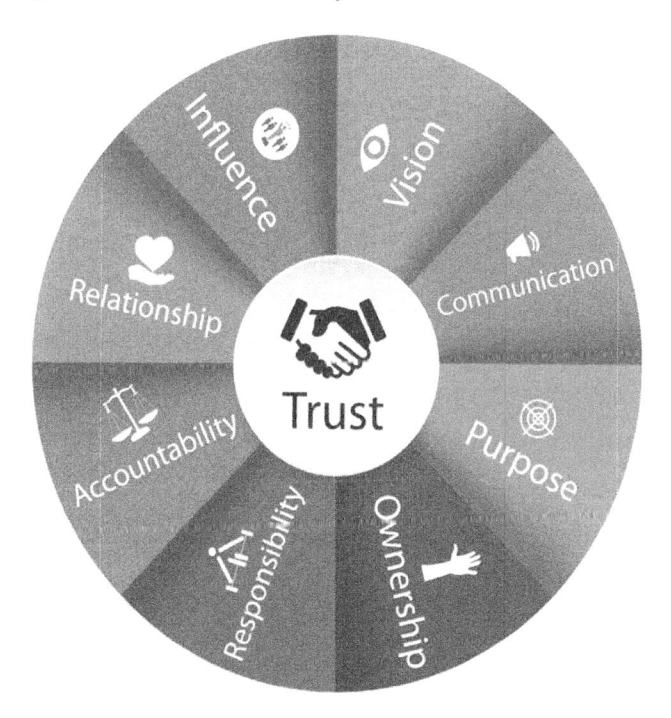

Consider each element in order, going clockwise:

Vision: A leader must have a vision, and he or she will bring that vision to his or her sphere of influence. All people look to follow someone who knows where they are going, as long as they want to go there too. A great leader starts with vision instinctively. "I see where we need to go and I know the way. Follow me."

Communication: Communication is key to all successful relationships. It is especially true for leaders. People cannot read minds, so if a leader has a vision, he or she must communicate it to those involved. Communication breeds understanding and understanding is fundamental to the human condition. We all want to be heard and understood.

Purpose: Another way to express purpose is to ask, "Why? Why are we doing what you are asking us to do? What is the reason, the purpose, and the benefit of doing this?" Here, communication is key, so that all parties can work out any doubts, fears, or misunderstandings before the mission gets too far along. Clarity of vision is the outcome you're looking for here. Everyone has a very clear understanding of where they are going and why. They have been heard and their concerns addressed.

Ownership: Everyone involved in the mission needs to feel some connection to it. Even more than that, everyone involved needs to know that they own a part of it. This is why it's so important to have open communication and clarity of vision. If you have an ownership stake in something, you are much more likely to care more and to work harder toward the success of the project. Without ownership, there is nothing to gain and nothing to lose, so why even care? It's critical that everyone involved in the mission have, and commit to, their share of ownership.

Responsibility: For there to be great and effective leadership, each person involved in a project must take responsibility for the outcome. It cannot be left to the person or the people "in charge." If there is clarity of vision, that vision will be well communicated and everyone's concerns will have been heard and addressed. And everyone will know the "why" behind the mission with a clear understanding of his or her ownership stake in the outcome. Then he or she are much more likely to take the required level of responsibility to see the task through.

Accountability: Of course, with responsibility comes accountability. Responsibility, as I have written about earlier in this book, refers to one's ability to provide an appropriate response or the ability to respond in an appropriate way. I see that as saying, "The way I will respond, given what I know, is that I will commit to doing the things I said I would do, the things I have agreed to do, and to do my part to ensure the success of this endeavor." Accountability is the measurement of that commitment. It is putting yourself out there by saying that you will do it and that you will be accountable for it by a particular time and measured to a certain agreed upon standard. It's a significant component, because otherwise the mission could be derailed by procrastination and good intentions.

Relationship: Great leaders take the time to develop relationships with the people they lead. It's not enough just to communicate with the group as a whole. The great leader must take the time to get to know what's important to each team members and what it is that motivates them as individuals. For some, it could be money. For others, it could be recognition. For yet another, it could be achievement or advancement. Everyone is motivated by something, and the great leader takes the time to find out what that is. And he or she also makes the effort to let each person know that he or she actually cares about that person, individually as a person, not just as a cog in the machine. When doing this, the great leader will build a sense of loyalty and commitment that cannot be bought and sets the stage for a level of teamwork that is hard, if not impossible, to create otherwise.

Influence: After the leader has implemented all of the elements listed above and everyone is on the same page, knows where they stand, understands what's expected of them, and knows his or her part and their stake in the outcome, then the leader is in a position to bring their influence to bear on the team to inspire them to do their best. Influence fills the void after control, seen as power, has been handed to the team members. Once empowered, and knowing that the leader cares individually for him or her and his or her most important values, a team member will usually exceed all expectations. When team members are properly motivated, the leader then only needs to bring his or her influence to the situation. As the cycle continues, the great leader accumulates credibility and his or her influence increases. The idea of being a boss is no longer appropriate because the great leader took the time and the care to cultivate the team members and paid attention to the elements required to achieve great results.

Trust: Ultimately, no leader will be effective or successful without the trust of the people he or she is trying to lead. That is the core foundational value involved in great leadership. All the elements in the illustration revolve around trust because, without it, the elements are hollow functions. Trust is foundational to all situations of leadership, whether in the home, the office, with your clients, or in the community at large. People need to see the real you and believe what you say. They need to know that what they see is what they will get and that you will do what you said you would do and you will finish what you started. Once you volunteer for something, it becomes a commitment. It's no longer optional. Once you commit to leadership, you must become the example and stick to the elements of great leadership described in the wheel. That is, that is what must happen if you expect great outcomes.

You can apply this wheel to your own mission, your own what. You don't need to have a team of people to lead in order to behave like a leader. Good leadership is a mindset, a mentality. It's how you choose to look at yourself. Can you articulate your vision? Can you have honest communications with yourself? Can you define your why and take ownership, responsibility, and be accountable to your own mission? Of course you can, and you will when you start seeing yourself as a leader and shifting your mindset.

Okay, what's left? Relationship and influence. You certainly do have a relationship with yourself, and you can take good care of that. Trust yourself and be honest with yourself. Rely on your purpose and your definition of success as you see it. Believe in yourself and love and accept yourself for who you are and who you are becoming. Choose where you get your influences and be discriminating. Sing your song, dance your way, and follow your vision. Realize your dreams. You have all that you need now. Because now is all there ever is. It's time to step up.

Before Moving On, Ask Yourself . . .

1. Where are three areas where you can "step up" as a leader to make a positive impact?

   _____
   _____
   _____
   _____

2. Who in your life do you feel needs your leadership?

   _____
   _____
   _____
   _____

3. Which leadership skills do you feel you naturally have and are prepared to use for positive change?

   _____
   _____
   _____
   _____

* Institute for Professional Excellence in Coaching ® Used with permission.

CHAPTER 10

You've Earned the Right to Have High Altitude Conversations

"Knowledge speaks, but wisdom listens."
- Jimi Hendrix

Everything I have written about to this point has been focused on how to gain a better understanding of how you think, how you perceive things, and how that impacts you in terms of helping your clients, getting better in your job, and getting the most out of your life. You are likely doing great right now, and others may even consider you to be quite successful. You have probably done some very impressive things with your life so far. Or you may be struggling and searching for a deeper understanding of what is holding you back from the success or happiness that you want. I suspect that the reason you picked up this book had something to do with the fact that you know deep down inside that you haven't achieved all of what you know you can achieve. And that's such a normal way to feel. Everyone has insecurities, fears, and feelings of not being good enough or not deserving of what you have or what you want. That's called being a human being.

I have written about the inner blocks we all have and how they can be managed to free you up from the limiting beliefs that hold you back. I have written about the impostor complex, which so many of us struggle with but somehow manage to overcome, just like so many other successful and well-known people do. I have outlined for you the levels of attitudinal perspective and how you can learn to shift your perspective to control your response in everyday life and in stressful situations. And I shared with you how to set and achieve goals, manage change, adopt a success mindset, and integrate leadership into your life. But these concepts and tools will only be effective if you can come to believe that you deserve success as you define it. They will only work if your definition of success is aligned with your values, and you are crystal clear as to your mission and your purpose in life. Or as Simon Sinek calls it, "Your why." As Roy Disney said, "It's not hard to make decisions when you know what your values are."

The High Altitude Conversation—You've Earned the Right

I've long believed that if you hold out as wise, you will attract those seeking wisdom. And as I grew in my advisory career, that was a principle that would underlie much of what I did.

I know, though, that it is challenging for some people to feel that they are "qualified" enough to start sharing their wisdom and conducting their business with a High Altitude View. But by virtue of the fact that you have read this book and that you truly seek the best for your clients and the other people in your life, you have earned the right. All of the "issues" that I have written about here, and with which all of us as humans deal, are also the things that your clients face in their lives. They want and need help with these issues as much as you do. Just being more self-aware, as you now are, qualifies you to ask the deeper questions and to take your clients and loved ones to the higher-level goals in their lives. In fact, you are uniquely qualified because you yourself have taken the time and have started doing the work to better understand yourself.

The truth is that you cannot ask your clients to do what you have not done, and you cannot ask your clients to go deeper than you yourself have been. That is why it's key that you constantly seek to deepen your understanding of yourself and the people in your sphere. You have to be living what you're teaching your clients. You have to be willing to do what you're asking others to do. For you to do better, you need to be better. To be better, you need to continually become more self-aware and gain enough confidence to show up in every situation as your authentic self. When you can do that, you will attract the clients you really want.

I read somewhere recently that the truth is, people who lack self-knowledge not only suffer spiritually, but professionally as well. In a recent *Harvard Business Review* article, the entrepreneur Anthony Tjan wrote, "There is one quality that trumps all, evident in virtually every great entrepreneur, manager, and leader. That quality is self-awareness. The best thing leaders can do to improve their effectiveness is to become more aware of what motivates people."

Embody what you teach because the unpopular truth is, you attract *who* you are, *not* what you want.

Don't Just Listen—Hear!

As a child, I was often told that the reason God gave us two ears and one mouth was so that we could listen twice as much as we speak. Isn't that the truth! But unfortunately, most people don't follow that rule. In fact, the ratio is usually the opposite. When you speak, you aren't learning anything. But when you listen, you have the opportunity to gain valuable knowledge—knowledge that can help you and your prospects, clients, and loved ones. But just listening isn't enough. You need to really hear what people are saying.

Too often the biggest problem in communication is that we don't listen to understand. We tend to listen to reply. I have been on many joint calls with other advisors where the advisor somehow manages to be quiet and "listen" to the client, only to follow with a barrage of information laid on the client as a response. These advisors thought listening was just waiting for their turn to talk again.

There is a technique I use in coaching called echoing, or feedback. I repeat back what the client or prospect said to me and ask a confirming question such as, "What I heard you say was this. Is that what you said?"

If the client responds affirmatively, then it means that I actually heard what the client said. If not, then I will ask him or her to clarify what was said so that I can be sure that I heard what he or she really said to me. I am not simply waiting for my turn to talk again. I am working to hear what was said and truly understand it. From there I can start asking questions to elevate the conversation to the highest level, or highest altitude view.

By the way, when asking questions in this process, work to ask open-ended questions. Many sales people are taught to ask closed-end questions to seek agreement. Closed-end questions usually beg for a response of yes or no. "You don't want to die and leave your family broke do you?"

"No, of course not!" the prospect will respond.

Nothing was really learned in that example. An example of an effective open-ended question would be, "If you were to die suddenly, what would you want for your family?"

The response is likely to reveal the prospect's true feelings as well as his or her deepest fears. You may follow up with, "Why is that important to you?" or, "Tell me more about that."

When we ask open-ended questions we learn, and when we learn we can help people.

Also, be careful when asking "why" questions, as they can be taken as sounding judgmental. "Why did you do that?" (The implication here is, "You dummy!") "What was your thinking there?" might a better way to check on the motive.

When you ask open-ended questions, you demonstrate to your prospect or client that you are truly interested in hearing what they have to say and in understanding what is most important to them. That is taking your client to their highest-level goals. That is having a High Altitude Conversation.

Always remember, salespeople sell products and services, generalists sell their time and knowledge, but High Altitude advisors share their expertise and wisdom.

Getting Honest with Yourself

By now you may have realized that no product, company, fancy office, or any other tangible, material thing will get you what you want in life. It really just comes down to your gaining the best understanding of who you are, what you want, and why you want it. This requires that you be willing to adapt and to let go of old beliefs that are actually keeping you from what you want. And it takes some courage to hold your ground and do the things that you know are best for you and those you care about.

Dan Sullivan, The Strategic Coach, talks about focusing on your Unique Ability®, those things that are most natural to you and take almost no effort to produce. Then he says to delegate all other functions to others. I believe this is an excellent concept.

I break it down like this: A-B-C-D.

- A is for artistry—a superior skill that you can learn by study and practice and observation, as in "the art of conversation"—specifically the art of having High Altitude Conversations.

- B is for boundless enthusiasm—an intense emotion-compelling action that is deeply stirring and an eager interest in or admiration for a cause or activity. This implies an energetic and unflagging pursuit of an aim or devotion to a cause, such as seeing that your clients and loved ones get all the things in life that they desire. This is accomplished by focusing on your highest-level goals and those of your clients.

- C is for CANI—*c*onstant *a*nd *n*ever-ending *i*mprovement, or betterment or refinement. This is consistent growth and expansion in all areas of your life—spiritually, mentally, emotionally, physically, and financially. This is never settling for things as they are, and always seeking to improve yourself and focus on progress. This gives you a deep sense of well-being, happiness, joy, and satisfaction.

- D is for drive—the energy and determination to set and achieve goals that you are enthusiastic about and that serve you and your values. This is instinctive to you.

Here is a winning formula:

A-B-C-D + HAV (High Altitude View) = Your Value.

When you provide value, you earn the right to get paid for who you are and what you bring to the relationship. If you can focus on your highest-level goals and those of your clients, and you can recognize when you are operating within A-B-C-D in all aspects of your business and your life, then you can feel confident to delegate, outsource, and automate all other functions in your business. All you have to do is to be the authentic you.

I want to share a poem called "I Create"* that a coaching peer, Will Rezin, wrote. He has a unique sensibility, and I want to share the poem because it very elegantly illustrates how each of us creates our own reality.

I CREATE.

With each thought I think… With each emotion I feel…

I create my life.

I create my day.

I create my relationships.

I create my success.

I create my joy.

I create everything in my world.

When I'm afraid, I create with my fear.

When I'm happy, I create with my happiness.

When I'm in love, I create with my love.

When I believe, I create with my belief.

I create my perception of the world.

I create my possibilities in the world.

Every moment of every day I am actively creating my life.

Know that you are creating this.

Your experience of this.

Your perception of this.

Which becomes your version of this.

Which becomes "this" to you.

And "this" is real, because you created it.

What are you creating?

I love this poem because it reminds me that we have full control over what we think, feel, and see. We have control over how we respond, how we treat others, and how we treat ourselves. If you are waiting for something to come along and change you, you may be waiting a long time.

I include it here to refocus you on what we started with, and that's the idea that everything comes down to your being truthful with yourself and truly understanding your values, who you are, what you want, and why you want it. You hold the key—no one else. You have earned the right, but you must take responsibility and you must do the work. And keep doing it.

How you do anything is how you do everything, and how you see anything is how you see everything. Shift your perspective, and you will shift your life and your outcomes.

You Are Already Enough

As you come to the end of this book, there is one message that I want you to take away, even if you don't remember a single other thing you've read. And that is, you are already enough!

Today, right now, who you are is enough. You can be one of the top advisors in the world dealing with the highest-level clients you can imagine, and you can do that today without being anything other than your current self. Having confidence in knowing that is all you really need. If you can just muster the courage to be you, that will be good enough for you to have everything you want in life.

That's partly because one of the core values for success in business and in life is a true caring for other people. And you have that in spades. If you didn't, you wouldn't be where you are today. You probably wouldn't even be in the financial services business if that weren't true.

Another reason it's true is because people, be they high-level clients, employees, associates, or family, all want the same thing from those they seek to trust, and that thing is authenticity. They want a real person. They don't want a person who is trying to impress them or is telling them what they want to hear. They want to know who you really are. And guess what, they can see you for who you really are, even if you haven't accepted that yourself. So please don't spend another moment trying to be anything other than who you really are, warts and all.

The Ruby Slippers

In the American film classic *The Wizard of Oz*, the main character, Dorothy Gale, gets swept away from her home in Kansas – farmhouse and all—by a tornado, during which debris knocks her unconscious. When she wakes, she is in a fairy tale land called Oz. A good witch named Glinda soon points out to Dorothy that she is now wearing a special pair of shoes that hold incredible power. The shoes are ruby slippers that fit Dorothy perfectly. Glinda tells her that the shoes had belonged to another witch, who was killed in the storm by the very same falling farmhouse in which Dorothy resided when landing in Oz. Glinda warns Dorothy that yet another very bad witch, sister of the dead witch, hoping to soon acquire the shoes for their massive power, will soon be coming to look for them. Glinda warns Dorothy to beware of this witch, and naturally Dorothy is terrified.

Before landing in Oz, Dorothy had been a bit unhappy living in Kansas and was looking to get away, thinking that the grass was greener on the other side of the fence. And now, she has indeed been swept away to a new and fantastic land that is so magical and mysterious, yet fraught with obstacles. And she eventually runs into that bad witch, on more than one occasion, who as it turns out can't even touch the slippers, let alone wear them.

This doesn't go over well with the bad witch who tries to kill Dorothy for the shoes, to no avail. After all the adventures and run-ins with the bad witch, Dorothy decides she wants to go back home and that maybe Kansas isn't so bad after all. She meets a few interesting characters along her journey—the Tin Man, the Cowardly Lion, and the Scarecrow—and with them, she seeks out the help of the Great Wizard of Oz, who she hopes will help her get back to Kansas. Dorothy and her new friends, who all have their own special requests for the Wizard, finally find the Wizard and are able to meet with him to seek his help.

He summarily dismisses them. They are all devastated.

But Dorothy isn't about to give up. At this point she has had enough of Oz and the wicked witch and she desperately wants to return to Kansas. Eventually, it comes to light that the great and powerful

Wizard of Oz is a mere mortal, a medicine man who himself is stranded in Oz. Contrary to Dorothy and her friends' belief, he has no special powers, but he does have one very important thing. He has wisdom.

The Wizard tells each of the characters that the things they are asking for are already present within each of them—courage for the Cowardly Lion, a brain for the Scarecrow, and a heart for the Tin Man. They just couldn't see it because they were too busy looking for it outwardly. He is indeed a wise man.

And what about Dorothy? She just wants to go home, back to her simple life and the friends and family she loves. She wants to go back to just being herself.

The Wizard makes a strong effort to help Dorothy, and tells her that the only way to get her back to Kansas is for him to accompany her in a hot air balloon. Unfortunately, Dorothy's dog Toto jumps from the balloon as they are preparing for takeoff. Dorothy makes chase, gathers Toto in her arms, and heads back to the balloon to rejoin the Wizard. But before she gets back, the balloon is untethered and begins to float away, heading back to Kansas with only the Wizard aboard.

A despondent Dorothy believes that she's now stuck in Oz forever, but soon Glinda returns to the scene. Dorothy pleads with her for help, and Glinda tells her, "You don't need to be helped any longer. You've always had the power to go back to Kansas."

Upon hearing that, Dorothy is incredulous and the Scarecrow asks Glinda, "Then why didn't you tell her before?"

Glinda responds, "Because she wouldn't have believed me. She had to learn it for herself."

When the Tin Man asks Dorothy what it is that she's learned, Dorothy says, "Well, I—I think that it—that it wasn't enough just to want to see Uncle Henry and Auntie Em—and it's that—if I ever go looking for my heart's desire again, I won't look any further than my own backyard. Because if it isn't there, I never really lost it to begin with! Is that right?"

Glinda confirms that this is indeed correct, and as it turns out, all Dorothy needs to do to get back home is to click together the heels of her ruby slippers three times and repeat the words, "There's no place like home . . . there's no place like home . . ." and then she will be transported back to Kansas. She does exactly that and wakes up at home in Kansas surrounded by the people she loves and her beloved dog Toto.

Why do I share this synopsis of this classic film? I share it because I experienced this same phenomenon in my own life. I struggled and constantly looked for all the answers to my problems, challenges, and insecurities to be solved by some outside solution. Maybe it would be better software, more sales ideas, a fancy car, better clothes, or a bigger office. Maybe if I bought a lead generation service I could make more sales. Maybe a client seminar series would help me overcome my fears and feelings of not being good enough. Maybe if I changed my company affiliation, things would be easier. But eventually I learned that I myself was wearing the ruby slippers all along. I just needed to learn it for myself. I eventually realized that all people wanted from me was for me to be my authentic self –the person who they knew cared about them and in whom they could trust. The guy *they* saw eventually became the guy that *I* saw. I had the power all along, but I was spending way too much time looking for it on the outside, when all along it was always there just on the inside.

When you come to realize this for yourself, you will find that you can accomplish pretty much anything you want in life without violating your principles and values and without violating anyone else's. You will gain an inner sense of confidence when you are aligned like this, and that nagging feeling that you feel now, that something needs to change, will go away.

But first, you will need to make some changes. You'll need to make some changes in the way you see the world, changes in the way you respond to change itself, and changes in the way you feel about yourself.

The whole idea of the High Altitude View is that your perspective creates or sabotages your path to success. You'll continue to attract the experiences you need to learn from until you get the lesson and make the shift in your perspective and adopt the thinking I have outlined in this book. When *you* show up differently in your relationships and your actions, your clients and those you care about will respond differently as well.

The only difference between you and someone who qualifies for the Top of The Table is that Top of the Table producers are willing to make changes—permanent changes—to get to where they want to go. What got you where you are today won't get you where you want to go tomorrow, so you must make some permanent changes. That's the only difference; it's not easy, or necessarily convenient, but it is required. TOT producers incorporate these changes into their everyday practices, and they maintain a High Altitude View and a success mindset. They work on their self-awareness and stay focused on what they can control.

Rory McElroy, a world-class professional golfer from Ireland who is at the top of his game in the professional golf world, recently won the 2019 TPC Championship. He has been playing at a very high level but hadn't won in his past ten significant events until this event. During a pre-round press conference, a reporter asked about his mindset. "Do you focus on winning?" someone asked.

His response was interesting. "I don't even know how to play the game and focus on winning. I have no idea what that even looks like. I just focus on each shot, trying to do my best and hoping for the best outcome."

Further, someone in the media asked him how he prepared then for his competition week to week. He replied, "Patience, perspective, preparation, and practice and this week that resulted in a win. So I guess four Ps equals one W."

I love that so much! If you could get so focused that you just paid attention to each shot, each meeting, each interaction, hoping for the best outcome each time, think about how simple your life could be. Patience, perspective, preparation, and practice—how simple! Respond versus react, take the High Altitude View, ask great questions, put others first, and become a great leader. Master the change game. You can do it.

In my life, I am all about perspective. I encourage people to try and look at their situations from different angles, different viewpoints. I try to impress upon them that they can choose their own filters, prisms, attitudes, and energy.

I've learned to accept and embrace my contrarian way of seeing things, not necessarily always believing what is being presented to me. This is important because this is my unique gift and just because it makes me different, it doesn't have to be a liability. In fact, I learned that it's a tremendous asset. The benefit to my clients is that they know I will challenge conventional thinking and will look all around a particular issue to ensure we get it right. I will ask probing, open-ended questions, questions from a High Altitude View.

How do you go about doing this? By adopting the mindset of the High Altitude View. Why do it? Because it helps you and your prospects, clients, and loved ones get aligned with your core values, and together you will be working to help them understand who they are, what they really want and why they want it.

And you will then be their trusted advisor and their leader.

Will this work for you in all aspects of your life? Maybe, maybe not. In my experience, this is what you'll find:

- Some will love it.
- Some will hate it.
- Some will block you.
- Some will help you.
- Some will accept you.
- Some will reject you.
- Some will judge you.
- Some will follow you.
- And some will not follow you.
- But in the end you will be true to yourself.

So please have the courage and the fortitude to just be you.

Can I ask you something? How much time have you already spent thinking about all the things you want in life? How many times have you written down your goals without ever taking action? How many times have you thought or realized that you'd be better off acting but never took action? Or worse yet, realized it was too late?

You know what's more powerful than thinking? Deciding. Now that is a powerful concept—deciding, and not looking back. When you go from merely thinking to deciding, your whole life changes. So why do people think things through and never make a decision accompanied by action? Maybe it's because they get stuck in "thinking limbo," because every good thing in life costs you something. It might cost you time, money, energy, a way of life, or a certain level of comfort to which you've become accustomed. It could cost you a piece of your identity that you've held onto for a long time. It could cost you all of those things.

But here's the reality—you can't achieve the things you want in life without sacrificing and deciding to go all in.

I am passionate about supporting and encouraging financial advisors and leaders in the financial services business to be their best selves. I work with advisors to help them align their core values with their businesses and life missions. My definition of success is helping you embrace your strengths and talents and learn to live with purpose and intention! Simply put, as a coach, my job is to take someone really good—someone like you—and help you break down that last wall so you can become great.

That's why I wrote this book. I wanted to share what I have learned with you so that you can reach your full potential and live your life with purpose and intention. If enough readers get to that place, think of the multiplying effect it will have in the industry, in the lives of your clients, and for their families. Think of how your gaining confidence in your authentic self will be so much more effective and powerful, and how your leadership will impact everything and everyone with whom you interact.

So decide. Decide to do the work, to make the changes, to commit to being your best self. And remember, how you do anything is how you do everything. How you see anything is how you see everything.

Take the High Altitude View. Change your perspective, change your life, and change your outcomes.

* *"I Create" is written by Will Rezin, a coach who tells others that he has dedicated his life "to understanding the science and philosophy of what motivates people, their behavior, and what creates the most extraordinary shifts in their lives." For more about Will Rezin, visit www.willrezin.com.*

Acknowledgements

The idea of writing a book had been rattling around in my brain for years. I knew it would write it eventually, but I kept putting it off, thinking that somehow it would just happen. Eventually, the stars aligned and a serendipitous email came into my inbox from a past acquaintance; someone who had interviewed me over the years for comments and contributions to the financial trade media.

"Ever thought of writing a book?' he asked in the email.

"Well, yes, as a matter of fact I have," I replied.

It just felt right and the timing was perfect. I don't think it's a coincidence that I received that email from Chuck Hirsch. (In fact, I don't even believe in coincidences.) And I am grateful to Chuck for all the hard work, vision, and focus that he brought to this project.

As it so happens, my father has written several books, and I always noticed how excited and proud he was to be working on each of his books. And when they were finally published, it was like he was showing off his latest great-grandchild. So thanks, Dad, for showing me the way and being a great example.

Of course, I want to give due credit to my loving and patient wife, Jan. Lord knows she was happy when this book was finally done, as she was the one who had to listen to me talk about each and every chapter, ad nauseum, every day. She never did anything but encourage me and support me and patiently listened, and for that I am very grateful.

I also want to acknowledge my kids, Stephanie, Michelle, and Ben. They have given me the awesome job of being their Dad, and the gift of being the grandfather of their beautiful kids. They have inspired me to be my best.

When I shared with my daughter Michelle that I was finally going to write a book, the subject came up as to what it was going to be about. "That's the thing," I said. "I don't really know yet."

Her response was priceless. "Well, it will be whatever it will be. Just write it; then you'll know."

What a liberating comment!

Throughout my life I have been blessed to have so many mentors, friends, and associates who contributed so much to my success and who truly cared about me and how I turned out in life. They shaped me, challenged me, and encouraged me. They gave me confidence, kept me grounded, and held me accountable. They are too many to list, but there are a few that I will mention. Jim Furton, my father-in-law, who passed way too early. He taught me that rules are not boundaries, but rather a point of departure, among other great things. George Wyland, my first insurance agent mentor, who taught me organization, persistence, and always shared his sense of humor and his belief in me. And my Uncle Lee Gillette who knew I could do more and be better, and who encouraged me to that end. He taught me so much about business, and I was able to take that with me when I finally started my own company.

I have had more friends than any one person deserves, and some who have always been there for me. Randy Scritchfield, Brian Heckert, Ed Skelly, David Berman, Scott Brennan, and Mark Schoenbeck are ones that immediately come to mind. Every one of these guys has been with me for the long haul though thick and thin. There are many others as well, including Rob Gawthrop, Greg Gagne, Taylor Sledge, and Jesse Rivera—the members of our awesome Million Dollar Round Table (MDRT) band Roundabout. Other influential MDRT friends who supported me and gave me opportunities that were life changing are Larry Fortenberry, Jen Borislow, Sarah Kaelberer, Ian Green, Dick

Sawyer, Ray Kopczynski, and Julian Good. I would also like to acknowledge my coach, Leanne Wild, for holding me accountable and for helping me stay focused on this project.

All of the people I have mentioned here have played some extraordinary role in my life, and this book has a little bit of each of them in it, as I have learned, borrowed, and shared so much with these people over my lifetime.

Much of the content, concepts, and viewpoints in this book are derived from my own life experiences and the interaction with my clients, associates, employees, mentors, and friends. But some ideas also come from and through concepts, learning, and training I acquired during my participation in the Strategic Coach® program, The Institute for Professional Excellence in Coaching®, (iPEC®), and my 31 years of active membership in the Million Dollar Round Table and the Top of The Table.

I have read countless books and witnessed literally thousands of motivational speakers during my lifetime. Credit is due to anyone whose quote, idea, or concept I have acquired and used, conveyed, modified, or shared during my 39-year career in the financial services business. Specific credit is noted within the book where appropriate.

It's quite possible that I have left someone important out of this acknowledgement, but rest assured this book would not exist but for the wonderful gift of support from all those people and organizations listed or inadvertently omitted. I only hope that this book will inspire you to take it upon yourself to mentor others, to be that great friend and influential family member, and to contribute to the great financial services business that has been so good to my family and me. Get involved, give back, and take your turn carrying the torch to make our great business and the world a better place for your children, your families, your clients, and the next generation of financial advisors.

About the Author

Steve Plewes is an experienced and effective communicator and problem solver. Having spent most of his life in the sales world, he has capitalized on his God-given skills for understanding people and helping them clarify and achieve their life goals.

He has developed transferrable skills, tools, and techniques that, when employed, enable professionals to increase their effectiveness and deepen client relationships.

As an independent business owner, Steve used his sales skills, creativity, and humor to build a successful relationship-based financial services career spanning nearly 40 years. Throughout his career, Steve has held a wide variety of leadership positions within the financial services business. He has been published and quoted in numerous media and financial trade publications and is a frequent industry speaker, having spoken from numerous main platforms at conferences around the world, including the main platforms of the Million Dollar Round Table and Top of the Table.

Steve brings this vast experience, wisdom, and unique insights to his work as a professional coach working with professionals in various fields to help them clarify and achieve their personal and professional goals.

Steve is passionate about helping people move forward in life. As a coach, he helps people gain clarity around their goals, identify and remove their blocks to progress, gain focus, and achieve growth with a sense of purpose and legacy.

Steve is a Life Member of the Million Dollar Round Table with 32 years of qualification including 14 Court of the Table and 11 Top of the Table qualifications.

Steve has been married to his wife and best friend, Jan, for 41 years, and they have been blessed with three children—Stephanie, Michelle, and Ben. They also have four beautiful and energetic grandchildren—Joanie, Frank, Callie, and Thea.

In addition to coaching, writing, and speaking, Steve enjoys playing guitar, practicing his photography, traveling, and playing golf with his wife and their friends.